Weaving in the Arts

Weaving in the Arts
Widening the Learning Circle

Sharon Blecher and Kathy Jaffee

HEINEMANN
Portsmouth, NH

Heinemann
A division of Reed Elsevier Inc.
361 Hanover Street
Portsmouth, NH 03801-3912

Offices and agents throughout the world

Library of Congress Cataloging-in-Publication Data

Blecher, Sharon.
    Weaving in the arts, widening the learning circle / Sharon
    Blecher & Kathy Jaffee.
        p.   cm.
    Includes bibliographical references (p. 177) and index.
    ISBN 0-325-00032-8
    1. Arts—Study and teaching (Elementary)—United States.
I. Jaffee, Kathy.   II. Title.
NX303.B64   1998
372.5'044'0973—dc21   97-51721
                                                     CIP

Consulting Editor: Thomas Newkirk
Production: Melissa L. Inglis
Cover design: Catherine Hawkes
Manufacturing: Louise Richardson

Printed in the United States of America on acid-free paper
02 01 00 99   RRD   2 3 4 5 6 7 8 9

To Marc, Joel, Jacob, and Ian,
weavers of the artistic tapestry of my life.
S. B.

To Mark, Sara, and Brian,
whose lives continue to "wonder me."
K. J.

Contents

Acknowledgments

Although this book was written by the two of us, it carries the spirit of a great many people. We thank all of them and, in particular, would like to mention some of them here.

We owe a deep debt of gratitude:

> First and foremost, to our students and their families for their trust and willingness to explore the possibilities with us.

> To our friends and colleagues, Gail Wood and Ray Levi, whose creativity and energy have enlarged our vision, and whose belief in the abilities of children have nurtured our souls.

> To Tom Newkirk for supporting and shepherding this book from first draft to final version.

> To Bill Varner and the rest of the editorial staff at Heinemann for their part in bringing this book to its final form.

> To Tom Romano for encouraging us to transfer our vision from idea to the printed word.

> To Joe Romano for helping us with photography.

> To Brett Rollins for donating his artistic talent in drawing the room layouts. Luckily, some things never change. Brett was one of the most cooperative of our second-grade students, and twelve years later he never skipped a beat when we asked for his help.

> To Melissa Ballard, Ray Levi, Marc, Ian, and Mark for their reading of early drafts.

To Chip Edelsberg and the Oberlin Board of Education for granting the sabbatical leave that provided the time to begin this project.

To the National Council of Teachers of English for awarding us the Teacher/Researcher Grant that provided the time and financial support to focus our research.

To the folks at the Center for Leadership in Education for their constant striving to validate the lives of teachers in general, and for their interest in our work in particular. Phyllis, you are special.

To our Oberlin colleagues in the classroom and in administration for their constant striving to help children make sense of the world.

And most of all, to our families because, more than anything, this book was born out of their love and support. They celebrated our triumphs, cheered us on when we were down, and ate countless takeout meals so that we could realize our dream.

Introduction

... those of us in the field of education are in the construction business and the environments and opportunities we create in our schools enable children, in turn, to create the kinds of minds they wish to own.   —*Eisner,* Cognition and Curriculum Reconsidered

Helping children to discover "the kinds of minds they wish to own" has been the cornerstone of our teaching philosophy and is the thread woven throughout the tapestry of the story we tell in this book. Our efforts to create a learning environment where the fine arts are the vehicles through which students can translate their beliefs about the world has provided valuable information for us about the ways children approach learning, and has heightened our appreciation of the different learning styles our students bring to that environment.

The seeds for this book have been germinating for a number of years, nurtured by the slightly nagging feeling that even in a language-rich, stimulating environment where most students were growing and thriving, there were still students who were not fully engaged, who were "living in the margins," so to speak, as though the fit wasn't quite right. It was a problem that kept coming at us, a puzzle that defied solution, until we began involving ourselves in the work of Howard Gardner, Elliot Eisner, and other educators who were thinking and writing about exciting ways to create curriculum that involved more than the traditional reading/writing/logical thinking approach to learning. The fine arts occupied a central place in the curriculum these educators were envisioning, an idea we found both exciting and validating because much of what we had observed in our classroom pointed to the fact that integrating the arts more fully into the curriculum might be the way to widen the learning circle.

We had always been aware, as many teachers instinctively are, that particular moments galvanize particular students. For the past several years we have been intrigued by the responses of our first- and second-grade students to the integration of the fine arts into our daily classroom curriculum. As opportunities to immerse themselves in music, movement, poetry, and the visual arts increased, we found more students becoming more deeply engaged in the learning process. As we have experimented with the use of music as a source for writing, dance as a response to reading or art, the creation of student operas as a response to story, and the development of artist workshops in which our students have had the opportunity of learning by getting inside the skins of artists and looking at the world through an artist's eyes, we have become increasingly aware of gains our students have made in their learning in general, and in their literacy learning in particular. We have seen children develop understandings about the making of meaning through art, music, dance, and poetry that they had failed to grasp through more traditional means.

As we watched these patterns develop we realized that we had been focusing with too narrow a lens. In our development of a language-rich environment the definition of *language* as reading/writing/speaking had been too confined. Our experience over the years had been telling us that encounters with the fine arts were becoming more central to the way learning was happening in our classroom. The work of Eisner and Gardner helped us crystallize that thought. The question we now began to ask was, "What if we enlarge the definition of language to include music, dance, poetry, and the visual arts?" Instead of language singular, what if we focused on the development of languages—what Elliot Eisner defines as "multiliteracy"?

These insights come at a time when a growing body of professional literature focuses on the development of multiple intelligences, teaching for understanding, broadening the definition of literacy to include art, music, and dance as valid expressions of that understanding, and the creation of stimulating environments that will enhance the thinking of students.

We hope to join that growing number of voices who speak of the arts as central to the curriculum, educators who see the arts not as extras to be addressed if there is time left over in the day, but as methodology, as valid ways students have of interpreting what they know and understand. But, in making a statement about thinking of the arts as methodology, let us be very clear about something: This is not a book about the *basalization* of the arts. It is not about the ways in which one can teach units by setting up centers for each of the intelligences, with students dutifully plugging their way through each one. When we speak of the arts as methodology we are referring to the creation of a classroom environment that will support the choice of music, dance, poetry, and the visual arts as natural expressions of understanding. It is a caveat we feel we must put forth at the outset because the arts are too important to our personal and professional lives to have our message misinterpreted.

Although the catalyst for this book was the combination of a semester's sabbatical leave the Oberlin Board of Education granted Sharon and an NCTE Teacher/Researcher grant we were awarded to pursue our question of the ways in which students are empowered in their literacy learning when the fine arts are woven into the daily classroom curriculum, it is actually the result of many more years of observation than just the one year devoted to the study. It has evolved out of specific moments in time that transformed our thinking: moments of reflection about our teaching, moments with children, moments with colleagues, moments with mentors; all moments that changed the way we view the world.

One of those moments is a memory of Renata, a sensitive, creative, private six-year-old, uncomfortable when attention was turned on her. Years later we can still see her that morning, sitting on the rug, cautiously raising her hand to take part in a discussion about animals and the way they move. Her voice, as she began to speak about her love of deer, was very small. But as she continued to explain why she was fascinated by the graceful way a deer leaps, her slender body rose into the most incredibly graceful arch and glided forward so that she *became* the deer of which she spoke. When she used her body to express her feelings, the transformation of this child was magical and, judging from the collective intake of breath from all of us who sat transfixed by what we had just witnessed, there was no doubt she had succeeded in communicating her message. Dance was at this child's center, her way of expressing ideas, and our curriculum would need to have ways to validate her approach to learning.

The book also grew out of the memory of a moment with Russell, another first-year student. Sandy hair, sunny disposition, open face with freckles dancing across the bridge of his nose, Russell was one of those kids who comes through the door each morning with his whole body reflecting an "I'm ready for anything!" attitude. That particular afternoon in late fall he had spent a major portion of the work period seated with pad and pencil, absorbed in the amaryllis that had blossomed only that morning. As we moved through the afternoon, reading with some children, holding conferences with others, answering questions and making suggestions, we would see him totally engrossed in his work. Finally toward the end of the day Russell came over to Kathy, handed her the paper that had occupied him for such a long time, and said, very simply, "What do you think, Mrs. Jaffee?" On the paper was the following:

Peik Padls fhlkring

Wetih Ael Thes Boudee it Lat
liek A Bndl of Hapepyness And Hot
peik padls fhlkekring in the Sun
And We Wattd for a laig
Teim And it Wes Wreh Weteing

Pink Petals Flickering

With all this beauty
It looked like a bundle of happiness.
Hot pink petals flickering in the sun.
We waited for a long time,
And it was worth waiting.

Russell, age 6

Touched by the sensitivity of this little boy, Kathy whispered, "Russell, you are a poet." You could almost see this child's view of himself expand as the truth of her statement struck home, and he replied in a voice full of wonder, " I really am . . . and I never knew I could do that!"

Again came the click of understanding that our learning environment had to have a place for the surprise and wonder that allowed children to make important discoveries about themselves.

It was moments like these that helped clarify something that perhaps should have been obvious all along. Even though we had developed a rich program of which we were justly proud, we had always been bothered by the discrepancy between what we were seeing in the classroom and what we knew was still possible. As we thought out loud about those times that our classroom and students seemed most alive, times when we were most satisfied by the fit between our vision and reality, when there was an energy in the air that was palpable, we realized that it was when we allowed our love of the fine arts to infuse our work.

We were people who had grown up with a passion for the arts. Kathy had studied ballet for years, so that a love of dance was truly a part of her. Sharon's knowledge and love of art, the result of years of roaming through museums from the time she was a child, was evident in the animated way she shared the latest art book she had discovered, or the delight with which she described her visit to Giverny. Neither of us was an accomplished artist, musician, or dancer, but we knew the power of the arts to change the way people felt about themselves and the world. We knew that our encounters with the arts helped us communicate our feelings and ideas. And now we understood that our passion for the arts had unconsciously shaped our vision, framed our teaching, and enveloped our students.

"Find out what you are interested in," writer Richard Lewis once said at a workshop, "it gives the children license to be interested." Sometimes what interests a person is so deeply ingrained that it takes a while to identify, but Richard Lewis was right on target with his advice. We have discovered that sharing ourselves and our passions with our students encourages them to explore their own interests and discover their own passions. The arts are wonderful vehicles for those explorations, and the elementary years are an ideal time to offer the broad range of experiences they make possible.

Visual memories have been one impetus for this book, but it has also evolved out of luminous moments of memorable language gleaned from expert mentors in countless workshops we have attended, books we have read, and conversations we have had, words that flowed into the core of our being, simmering and blending with our own thinking over the years until they developed into the philosophy that now guides our work. We quote many of these mentors throughout this book, partly because they illuminate our message, but also because we want to acknowledge the contribution they have made to our learning.

A word about the format we used in writing our story. The question most often asked by colleagues who attend our workshops is: "How did it all begin?" This book is an attempt to answer that question.

The four chapters that make up Part I deal with the development of individual aspects of our program. In Chapter 1: Building a Foundation, we try to begin at the beginning, showing how we set the stage and begin to establish the milieu in which learning will take place. Chapter 2: Creating a Languages-Rich Environment with Music and Movement illustrates how we have expanded the definition of language to include music, dance, poetry, and the visual arts, and shows how we begin to weave the threads of the fine arts into the daily curriculum. Chapter 3: Poetry Immersion is the story of how we reclaimed poetry as a natural response to learning, how we use imagery and metaphor to help children reinvent their thinking and expand their understanding of the world. Chapter 4: Art as a Visual Response is an explanation of the breakthroughs our students have made once we began to focus upon drawing for understanding.

Part II is devoted to a description of immersion workshops we have developed. Chapter 5: Artist Workshop, and Chapter 6: Opera Workshop are detailed accounts of the eight-week immersion workshops we have developed so that children can get inside the skins of creative artists and think about the unique ways these people approach learning. And finally, the Epilogue: Insights and Inquiries is a discussion of some of the insights we have developed, as well as some of the lingering questions that remain. The text is followed by extensive annotated bibliographies that we hope you will find useful.

There is a certain irony in using written language to try to explain a way of teaching and learning that has expanded the definition of language to include other forms of expression. Using words to talk about a child's artwork, movement experience, or musical understanding is a bit like reading the translation of a foreign language novel: Something gets lost. So we will do our best to work in the style of what ethnographer John Van Maanen (1988) terms "impressionist ethnographers" whose intention is "not to tell the readers what to think of an experience but to show them the experience from beginning to end and thus draw them immediately into the story to work out its problems and puzzles as they unfold" (143). We offer a detailed look into our classroom curriculum and environment because it may be easier to look at the broader issue of learning if we do it in terms of specific students, teachers, and places. Living with our curriculum has brought to light fascinating discoveries about children's learning, revealed interesting threads and patterns, and raised complex and provocative questions. Our findings are based on interactions with *our* students in *our* classrooms, but as Elliot Eisner (1991) points out in *The Enlightened Eye*:

> A qualitative study of particular classrooms and particular teachers
> in particular schools makes it possible to provide feedback to teach-
> ers that is fundamentally different . . . ways that are useful for under-
> standing other schools and classrooms and learning about individual
> classrooms and particular teachers that are useful to them. (12)

It is a journeyman's essay of many years of observing, exploring, experimenting, and studying to find the best ways to help children make sense of their world. Our hope is that some of what we say may trigger an idea that leads you to new discoveries about your own classroom community.

Part 1

Chapter 1

Building a Foundation

The way to establish a School for Children in each classroom is not to rush about filling the room with a variety of paper, bulletin boards, conference areas . . . but instead, to fill the room with children's lives.   —*Lucy Calkins*, Living Between the Lines

How does one build a community of learners in which each child feels a sense of belonging? How can one create an environment that is full, rich, and stimulating, yet safe enough so that children at all points along the learning continuum feel at ease pursuing their inquiries? How does one work within that classroom community to build a common language so that our learning becomes something we have constructed together?

Questions such as these have been the driving force behind our teaching ever since we first decided to team together over a decade ago. They are particularly important to us because of the diverse population that fills our classroom year after year. Oberlin is a study in diversity, a very small town with an influence and reputation that belies its small size. It is the home of Oberlin College, a school well-known for its rigorous academic program and for its liberal philosophy (it was the first coed and racially integrated college). It is also the home of the renowned Oberlin Conservatory of Music. Oberlin as a college town is the view most people seem to have, a perspective that brings with it a belief that the Oberlin School system is a college laboratory school.

But Oberlin College is only a part of the picture of diversity that characterizes this area. The town of Oberlin is set among the steel mills and factories of Lorain County and is ringed by farms. It was a major stop on the Underground Railroad in the 1800s, so many African Americans settled in the town and became an important part of the fabric of this community. The people of Oberlin—those who work for the Federal Aviation Agency (FAA) and Oberlin College (the two major employers in this very small town), those who own and are employed by the small businesses in Oberlin, and those who work in the factories and on the farms—range across broad racial, ethnic, socioeconomic, and academic spectra. Their children attend our very small school system of approximately 1300 students.

Our school system, like any other, is a direct reflection of the community. With all the diversity, the Oberlin schools are a wonderfully challenging and energizing place to teach in. Some of the students who enter our program in the fall have been abroad on sabbaticals with their parents before they have even entered kindergarten; others have never traversed the thirty miles of roadway that connect us to Cleveland. Some enter our first year reading on a fourth-grade level while others are barely at a kindergarten entry level. For some the preschool years have been filled with the kinds of rich experiences that translate well to the traditional view of school; others arrive with experiences that may be equally rich, but are not so easily accessed by traditional methods.

We began asking ourselves some hard questions when our beliefs about the ways children learn began bumping up against the fact that those children who enter school ready to translate their experience through reading/writing were at a distinct advantage in a traditional school culture, where these sign systems are a prime requisite for success and often are the only access offered. It is one thing to claim to value the individual learning styles of young children, but these words ring hollow when the traditional school culture sends a different message. We wanted to develop a program that would celebrate the diversity and would honor all of these children's stories. If we were going to make the classroom a more democratic place, we needed to enlarge the definition of language to include other ways of communicating understanding.

As we observed our students trying to make sense of the world we discovered that we could widen the learning circle by including music, dance, and the visual arts as valid ways for children to show their understandings. We began to create an environment where the arts would serve as bridges to that understanding. Working from our belief that in their early years children are ready to develop diverse ways of thinking about the world by studying the way experts think and work, we actively sought to create environments that would encourage our students to explore these modalities in a deeper way by literally immersing them in the specialized worlds of the artist and musician. Thus, for example, was born our idea for Opera Workshop and Artist Workshop, the extended immersion experiences in which the fine arts provide the curricular framework for our teaching and learning.

Our vision of a vibrant classroom community is grounded in collaborative work, ongoing dialogue, and shared understandings, all driven by children's questions. We teach together as partners, sharing a group of approximately forty-six first- and second-grade students who stay with us for two years.

The two years our students are with us provide an opportunity for them to explore many different ways of learning about the world, a time to discover the unique qualities in their own style of learning, and a chance to appreciate the equally unique contributions of their peers. We have structured the program around the following priorities and goals:

Priorities	Goals
collaborative work	sense of community
shared decision making	generative curriculum
process teaching/learning	problem solving skills
choice	self-direction
acceptance of responsibility	self-confidence
multiple ways of knowing	critical and creative thinking

To work toward these goals we have created a workshop environment infused with the fine arts and centered around focused studies generated by children's questions, an environment we have found conducive to a diversity of learning styles, and one that builds strong family partnerships.

We decided early on that if collaboration were to frame the work of our classroom, our teaching partnership would be a model for our students. The same reliance on close observation, discussion, and search for patterns that has enlarged our thinking as teacher/researchers now also guides our students' investigations. In other words, the model of investigation and observation leading to discovery of patterns that, in turn, lead to new investigations, is the working model for all members of our classroom community.

But how does it all begin?

It begins with the belief that the environment we create in the classroom must be a reflection of what is important in our students' lives. In order for that to happen we establish our first contact with families before the school year even begins.

We want our families to know that we value the knowledge they can share about their child's approach to learning, so as soon as class lists are finalized at the end of June we send a letter and survey to each child as well as a letter and survey to the parents or guardians. Although we try to keep this first communication low-key, we design it so that both children and parents can begin thinking about the contributions they can make to the classroom. The wonderings and interests of both students and parents are vital to our planning.

To build familiarity and security, we invite families to drop by a few days before the beginning of the school year. We encourage them to roam around the room, and to take a few moments to talk informally with us. Because the space in which we work is large (two classrooms with the center wall knocked out) and because it looks different (no teacher or student desks, but instead tables clustered into work areas) (see Figure 1.1) we know new students could be easily intimidated. Children and parents stop by throughout the day and often, when several families find themselves in the room at once, the children who are returning for a second year will automatically take the younger child in hand and show him around. It's a natural thing for them to do because leading visitors on tours of the room is the responsibility of the children all throughout the year.

Building a community of learners is of prime importance and takes priority as the school year begins. We know that time spent in learning about our

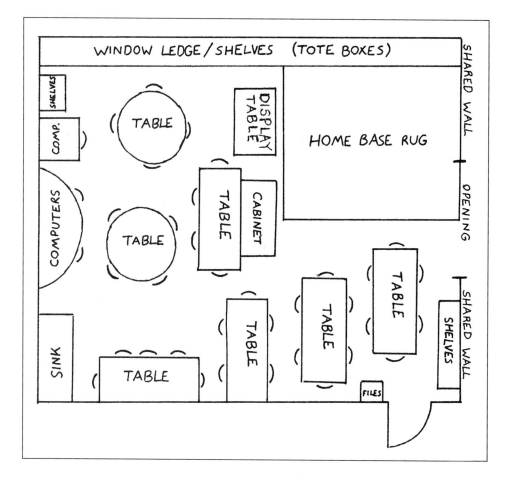

■ FIGURE 1.1A Layout of the room (two-part drawing)

students, children with whom we will be living and working for six hours a day, is time well spent. By taking the time to get to know each other's different gifts and needs, and learning to appreciate the diversity that abounds, we start to establish common ground, build a common language, and construct the first threads of a safety net of trust and caring that will allow all of us to take the kinds of risks that help learning go forward.

During the weeks preceding the opening of school we spend a great deal of time working on a daily schedule that will reflect our beliefs about the way children learn. (See Appendix A for a copy of the schedule.) Lofty goals about

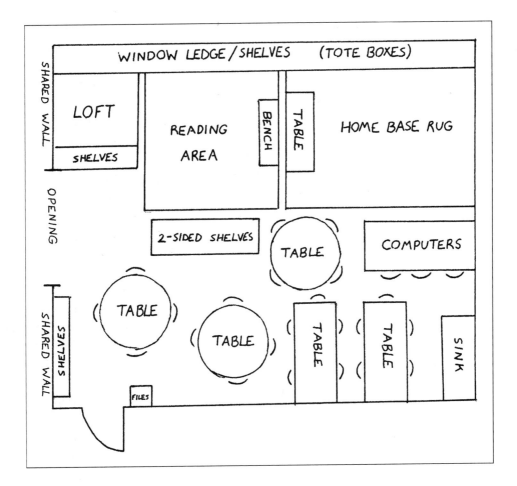

■ FIGURE 1.1B Layout of the room (two-part drawing)

discovery learning do no good if we segment the day into fifteen-minute time slots. We deal with the frustrations of working around set schedules such as "specials" (library, gym, music, art), but we work very hard to design the rest of the schedule to support our beliefs. Learning is a social endeavor with talk and collaboration at its heart. We leave many spaces for both formal and informal talk and collaboration. Some of the talk is in the form of dialogue, such as class meetings where we model teaching or discuss concepts; other times it is more of a conversation, as in literature circle discussions or science talks (an exciting approach to the teaching of science we first read about in Karen Gallas' *Talking Their Way into Science*).

Collaboration also takes many different forms, from the self-initiated pairing up of kids interested in the same idea to cooperative work that goes on in pairs or small groups during work periods and workshops. That collaboration can be student/student, as, for example, much of the work that happens at the discovery (science) area, or in math and writing workshops; it can be teacher/student, as in reading/writing conferences; or teacher/teacher, as in the type of collaboration we model when we plan our curriculum and workshops. We often talk to our students about the workshops we do, letting them know that it is their learning we share, and asking their opinions of what we should include.

Some of the teacher/teacher collaboration that takes place before the year begins involves talking about the concepts that will frame our work with our students, concepts such as life cycles, human relations, conservation, energy, and work. These are areas broad enough to include all of the objectives of the various courses of study, while leaving plenty of room to design the curriculum around the children's interests and questions.

Our initial focused study, planned for the first two weeks of the school year, has evolved out of the questions and reactions of many young students over many years. The idea of this study is to view the classroom as an anthropological site, using the tools and thinking of an anthropologist to uncover layer upon layer of information about the place where we will be working and the community in which we will be living. In *Listening In*, Tom Newkirk describes the classroom as a place where two cultures come together: the culture of the child and the culture of the adult, each with rich lessons to share with the other. It is a nontraditional but very powerful viewpoint that challenges the educator to find ways to build bridges between those two cultures.

Introducing the work of the classroom from an anthropological perspective excites us for many reasons. First of all, children enter a classroom with all sorts of questions and apprehensions about this place called *school*. Even our second-year students return wondering how things will have changed now that they are a year older. What better way to develop a sense of security than by validating and exploring those feelings and questions? We ask the children to consider such questions as:

What is this place called *school*?

What artifacts can you find that give us clues as to what people do here?

Are there enough materials (books, dictionaries, computers) so that there is one for each person?

What does that tell us about the way we work here?

The children search for one artifact to bring back (or point out if it is too large to transport) for discussion. The exploration time provides an opportunity for children to find their way about the room and to discover where things are stored and how space is used. Their explanations reveal a great deal about their expectations and understandings and give older students and us the chance to explain the ways these materials are used in our classroom. (It's also satisfying and a bit of a relief to hear how much the older children have absorbed during their first year in the room.)

Second, the tools of the anthropologist—inquiry, close observation, and a search for patterns—are the same ones that guide our work in the classroom. The investigations and explorations we plan during work periods those first two weeks, for instance, allow us to introduce data-gathering tools such as surveys and interviews. We encourage children to devise their own methods of recording information on these first surveys and graphs, much the same way we ask them to use functional spelling to get their thoughts down on paper. When the information is shared later in class meetings we talk about ways to look for trends and patterns.

Class meeting and work period time introduce our students to the many ways music, dance, poetry, and the visual arts will be woven into our work. At some of our initial class meetings we put on upbeat music (jazz is excellent!), make a circle, and introduce ourselves, creating a movement to go with our names. The name and movement is then repeated by everyone else in the circle. Nothing in this activity has to be forced, and even movements of the extremely shy child, such as rolling one's shirt, scrunching up one's face with indecision, or dropping one's head become that child's contribution to the game. When kids find their uncertainty accepted by the group, they begin to understand that the only place we *can* start is where we are.

We include many opportunities for movement during those first weeks, partly because we know that little bodies fresh from a summer of outdoor freedom need plenty of opportunity to move around, and also because we want to give the children the chance to feel the rhythms that are a natural part of us. "The rhythm of the heart is the first and most important rhythm of human life," writes Langston Hughes in a newly illustrated edition of *The Book of Rhythms*, adding "The rhythms of music start folks to feeling those rhythms in their minds and in their bodies" (1995, 6–7).

Since alphabet books teach us to recognize the rhythms that exist deep within us, they are our first reading genre. Alphabet books are extremely user-friendly. They do not threaten even the most tentative child, and they are an effective way to help children begin to internalize the rhythms of language. Reading Bill Martin Jr.'s *Chicka Chicka Boom Boom* aloud with your students, for example, without feeling the urge to dance around is virtually impossible. (Our suggestion is not to fight it; give in and dance. The kids [and you] will find it exhilarating!) Once kids are caught by the music and rhythm of the language of many alphabet books, you can continue to entice them with books such as Nancy Lecourt's *Abracadabra to Zigzag*, which introduces children to playing with language, or gems such as Mary Elting's *Q Is for Duck* or George Shannon's *Tomorrow's Alphabet*, which offer a different way of thinking about the alphabet.

A study of alphabet books also allows us to help some of our students take a second look at the familiar. Many of our more developed readers see themselves as beyond the alphabet genre until they get involved in books like Doubilet's *Under the Sea from A to Z*, Paul's *Eight Hands Round*, Wilk's *The Ultimate Alphabet*, or Viorst's *The Alphabet from Z to A (with Much Confusion on the Way)*. These books are quite complex in language and format and a real challenge for more developed readers.

During work periods, kids explore the various materials and tools they will be using in their work throughout the year. In the reading area, for example, children might find an old favorite to read alone, or to share with a friend. Our discovery area is set up so children can begin using sketching to develop their observational skills. We might ask them to sketch a plant by drawing everything they see and then looking one more time to find something they missed. As they draw pictures of things they feel are important in their lives in the art area we encourage them to try out different media (paint, markers, colored pencils). Math investigations encourage the exploration of various materials (pattern blocks, Cuisenaire rods, balance scales, learning links) and again we ask children to find a way to record their findings so that someone else will be able to interpret them. Blank paper for these explorations allows children to use whatever recording method makes sense to them, and gives us a chance to see how our students organize information. It is during these work period times that we move from group to group observing which children work easily in a collaborative situation and which will need a lot of guidance; which children stay engaged for long periods of time and which have short attention spans. We use this time to ask the kinds of questions of individual children that give us insights into the way they go about learning. And, most important, we begin to discover the diverse talents these children bring to their learning.

Our choices for read-alouds during these first weeks are also designed to help our students understand the things we value. The first book we read on the first day of school is *Together* by George Ella Lyon. It is a simple story poem about what can be accomplished when people work together, and it is a wonderful example of the sense of community we hope to foster. We begin reading it as a poem for two voices, but by the time the recurring pattern, "Let's put our heads together and dream the same dream," has come around the third or fourth time, the children are chiming right in. That first blending of all of our voices is always a special moment.

It is also important to us that we choose a special chapter book to begin reading at the end of each day. One that has utterly captured the imagination of our entire class is *I'll Meet You at the Cucumbers* by Lillian Moore. It is a fitting book to read during the first few days of school because it is the tale of a charming mouse named Amos who sees the world from a very unusual perspective. He is perfectly content in the country, observing everything about him, and writing down his "thoughts." But, like these young children, brimming with promise yet full of uncertainty, Amos knows there is a larger world out there waiting to be discovered. Finally, giving in to the pleas of his pen pal in the city, he decides to enlarge his view of the world. It is in the New York Public Library that Amos makes the most wondrous discovery about himself: The "thoughts" he has been writing are really poems! He is a poet!

Books such as this one seem to open up so much for our children. Nancy Willard once said at a conference, "Your own experience is not only what happens to you but anyone else's that you can imagine your way into." When we read a book like this one early on in the year we hope the children will see themselves in Amos and think about the possibilities the year holds, and the discoveries they will make about their own learning.

We also read shorter books such as George Ella Lyon's *Who Came Down That Road?* and *What If? Just Wondering Poems* by Joy Hulme so our students will begin to see the important place questions hold in our view of learning. *The Conversation Club* by Diane Stanley is a gently humorous way to lead into a discussion of the protocol for talk that we expect to establish for our literature circles and classroom discussions. We follow this with several class meetings during which we generate the guidelines that will make our classroom community a comfortable place for talking, learning, and living.

Finally, our class meetings during the first few weeks provide blocks of time to begin talking our way into becoming a community of learners. Our hope is that the distinct threads of the individual stories we each bring to the classroom in the fall will be woven into a rich tapestry that tells our collective story by the time school ends in the spring. We begin gathering those threads early on in the year, often during the first week of school, by asking the children to begin creating life boxes, an idea we got from reading Jane Fraser and Donna Skolnick's *On Their Way: Celebrating Second Graders as They Read and Write.*

We begin by reading Mem Fox's *Wilfred Gordon MacDonald Partridge* to the class, so that the children will get some idea of the types of things a life box might contain. We want to get to know these children who are new to us. What is important to them? What do they value? When they are asked to limit the artifacts they may include, what will they choose as most important? What does that tell us about them as individuals, as learners? What does it suggest as far as using a particular child's interests to help design his/her learning? What patterns emerge as children share life boxes that suggest interests around which to design curriculum that will stimulate this particular group? What feeling are we getting about this group as a whole? (During the year that rock collections, test tubes, batteries, computer innards, crystals, and myriad other science experiments showed up in one life box after another it became clear that we were going to have to design a heavy-duty science focus.) The questions proliferate as the children talk and share, and the more they talk, the more information we get about how to create an environment where each of these children is likely to find a place to thrive.

As we gather valuable information about our students, they are making equally valuable connections with each other. Through the children's talk mere acquaintances turn into friends. Ian launches into a spirited talk about his love of trains, displaying a truly impressive collection of both objects and facts, and several children excitedly respond by telling him of their own fascination with railroading. Marshall shares the wild animal and nature books that are his favorites, and several other budding naturalists begin to nod their heads in complete understanding. Abby speaks almost reverentially about her passion for horses, of learning to ride, of hoping someday to be a jockey, and the very next morning Michael, a very shy child, hands her a book about horses he has brought from home saying, "Here, Abby, I thought you would really like to read this." As the life box sharing continues, one can virtually see the bonds of friendship tighten between these children.

Finding common ground—taking valuable class time to put children and their lives center stage—fosters the belief that learning is, above all, about our lives. What is important to our students matters to us as teachers. What they think and feel and wonder about is central to what this place called *school* is all about.

Building a strong sense of partnership with parents is also of great importance to us. In addition to an open invitation to visit or work in the room, the bridge between home and school that the survey letters back in July established is reinforced with a family potluck picnic the first week of school. It continues to develop through parent workshops designed to address parent questions, and is maintained throughout the year through weekly homework assignments that contain a special section for parent comments. These comments provide information about how parents view their child's progress. They also use the section to ask questions or share concerns, so that the parent comment section of the homework becomes an ongoing dialogue and a valuable resource in planning our parent workshops. A discussion of just one special homework assignment may help to illustrate the richness that can result when such relationships are nurtured.

As part of a whole-school project adapted from Brian Lanker's photo essay *I Dream a World: Portraits of Black Women Who Changed America*, each class at Eastwood was asked to design a square to be sewn into an Eastwood quilt that would represent the children's hopes and dreams for the world. Each classroom was free to choose the subject for their particular square, and since our class had just completed a focus on families, surveying parents and grandparents and collecting family stories, we all decided that we wanted our square to show how important our extended families were in our lives. Our letter to families explained the project and included the following request:

> Please send in a small piece of material that has special meaning to your family. It should be a piece of material that has a story to tell.

The very next day a number of children returned their letters bulging with fabric pieces. We suspected we were in for something special with this project when we read the note James wrote to accompany his scrap of fabric:

> This is some of the matirel that my moms wetting maid wore.

> This is some of the material that my mom's wedding maid wore.

The letters and contributions that arrived day after day were wonderful, revealing stories that made our families so much more real to us. There were contributions—such as James' material from the bridesmaid's dress, or a piece of a jeans jacket worn the night mom met dad—that were reminiscent of times that set the stage for the beginnings of the family. There were letters that reminded the child of the anticipation with which his or her birth was awaited. Some contained a scrap of material from the maternity dress worn by mom; others told stories about first blankets or quilts, many of them made by special family members. Often these stories carried with them the idea of continuity. This one from Martin's family is typical:

> This quilt was begun before Martin was born and finished last
> week. Every child in his family did some of the quilting stitches on
> it, and lots and lots of love went into it and we have hopes that this
> first-generation quilt will be around for a long, long time.

There were stories about fabric of sentimental value that had gone into wash-cloths that had cleaned each child in a family, or towels used on a first trip to camp, or pillowcases that were, in Mary Kate's words, "the starting point for many of our dreams." There were remnants of first Halloween costumes, first performance outfits, and first school sweatshirts. And then there were the pieces of favorite pants and shirts, worn until they fell apart. One of our treasures was a scrap from a favorite shirt the child's grandfather still had from his college days!

A number of families celebrated the generational aspect of the project by sending scraps from quilts that had been handed down from great-grandparents, many of whom lived on in the history of the quilt; other families, like the one that sent a piece of a comforter used for nightly story times on mom and dad's bed, celebrated precious family moments worked into busy lives.

Some stories, such as the one about Ian's scrap of a pillowcase that he had imprinted with cows because he had once lived in Vermont and his last name was Cowley, made us chuckle with delight. Sarah's colorful material covered with a peacock pattern arrived with the story that her great-grandmother had been given this fabric to sew into curtains when she married into the Peacock family.

Other stories made our hearts ache. One such letter contained a piece of a baby washcloth that had been lovingly used on each child in the family and a note that said the cloth had originally been made for a child who had died in infancy.

Robert Coles, in his book *The Call of Stories*, comments that our stories *are* our lives. The outpouring of love and caring contained in those family letters made it clear to us that this was more than a school/family project, certainly more than a homework assignment. It had turned into an act of trust and sharing on the part of the families of these children, a sharing that strengthened the bond between us and made it that much easier to work together in this endeavor called learning.

Getting to know one another as people—taking the time to listen to each other's stories—helps students see learning as a community effort. Once that foundation is in place, creating an environment rich enough to speak to the unique style of each child is the challenge to which we turn.

Chapter 2

Creating a Languages-Rich Environment with Music and Movement

Kids: they dance before they learn there is anything that isn't music.
—*William Stafford*

Classroom life revolves around communication. As the children become comfortable with the classroom setting we encourage them to express that communication in many different forms.

One of those avenues is through the written and spoken word. We celebrate words. Every time we share a beautifully written book with the children we take the time to talk about wonderful words we have heard—words that roll around inside our mouths. We want to introduce our students to the kinds of words Maya Angelou describes in her poem "I Love the Look of Words" (in Feelings, 1993), words that come . . .

> snapping from the page. Rushing into my eyes. Sliding
> into my brain which gobbles them

We revel in such words during read-aloud times, when we share marvelous and mysterious books like Margaret Mahy's *17 Kings and 42 Elephants*. We play with the alliteration of phrases like "Tinkling tunesters, twangling trillicans," "moist and mistalline," or "bibble-bubble-babbled to the bing-bangbong." We laugh over the heavy sound of "proud and ponderous hippopotamums" and delight in the image of tigers "drinking lappily." Words such as these are not lightly dismissed; they delight the eye, ring in the ear, and play on the tongue. They help us understand how valuable words are in the real world, how those who become comfortable with them open themselves to marvelous possibilities in their learning.

Comfort with the spoken word makes it possible to play around with ideas, adds a personal voice to decision making, and solidifies a place in the classroom community. Class meetings help children learn to articulate their ideas. In those meetings where we model a lesson or give directions, children learn to listen critically and ask for clarification if they don't understand something. In discussions such as book talks or science talks, we try to stay in the background so that the talk is more of a conversation among the children. Restraining ourselves from repeating or paraphrasing what individual children say has been difficult, and we are still tempted to jump in and clarify a point more often than we would like to admit. But we realized that when, in an attempt to move the discussion forward, we paraphrased a child's incomplete statement or repeated an inaudible comment, we were teaching our students to listen to us, not to each other. Not surprisingly, there has been a direct correlation between the decrease in our voices and the growth in the ability of our students to focus on each other's words, to clarify their meaning when their peers don't understand them, and to speak in a voice that can be heard. Book talks and science talks have also taught children to respect the opinions of their peers, to listen carefully so they can build upon each other's ideas, and to acknowledge the contribution a classmate has made to their thinking.

Ease with the written word gives voice to our students in a different way. Words are celebrated when we respond to a child's first attempt to leave a message in functional spelling on our message board. It is a communication center replete with examples of children using writing effectively.

The message left by Madeleine on the first day of school let us know right at the outset what she felt to be important (see Figure 2.1).

There was Russell's message, also left during the first week of school:

> Dear Miss Jaffee
> I thik I hav to mohc wrk to do in SchooL. kan we have a coon-
> frins to Gatr?
> Love RUSSell

> Dear Mrs. Jaffee,
> I think I have too much work to do in school. Can we have a con-
> ference together?
> Love, Russell

His no-nonsense request told us that he believed us when we said his needs were important, and he had certainly internalized the structure for solving problems!

■ **FIGURE 2.1 Madi's note**

Some messages, such as this one left by Emily, are an acknowledgment that we learn to know each other well, and that readers share their excitement about books with other readers.

> Dear mrs. Blecher
>   I cod not reesist in writing a leter to you. I fowd to book's on rocks at the liyberiry in town they wher calld *Rocks and Rock Collecting*, *Rocks and Minerals* and you know I loke rocks
>   Love Emily

Dear Mrs. Blecher,

I could not resist in writing a letter to you. I found two books on rocks at the library in town. They were called *Rocks and Rock Collecting*, and *Rocks and Minerals*. You know how I like rocks.

Love,

Emily

Some communication, such as Bryce's guilt-inducing message showing a tiny child lost on an enormous class meeting rug (see Figure 2.2), are eloquent proof that a picture is worth a thousand words, and it made us think twice about taking a personal day early in the year.

Written and spoken language is also an important part of reading/writing workshop. Others have written extensively on the connection between reading and writing, genre studies, and the importance of choice in the teaching of reading and writing. Our purpose here is not to go over that ground; rather, it is to convey the feel of the reading/writing workshop environment, and to demonstrate how all the imagistic language, reading as writers, and genre studies seep into the children's consciousness and prepare the ground for the art and opera immersion workshops described in Part II.

Whether the book being read during reading/writing workshop is a student choice or a teacher choice, we try to make sure that the books available will help our students "fall through the words into the story," as Jane Yolen quoted in one of her talks. For our read-alouds we often choose books that contain vivid metaphors. In *Dear Rebecca, Winter Is Here*, Jean Craighead George describes time as "little hands of darkness":

In summer they began bringing winter. They pulled the night over the edges of the dawn and dusk and made the days shorter.

Diane Siebert begins *Mojave* with the majestic lines:

I am the desert.

I am free.

Come walk the sweeping face of me.

After hearing us read this book and then reading it many times on her own, Anna Claire wrote on her reading self-assessment:

One story I really liked was *Mojave* because it has beteful paintings in it and the words sounded wonderful in your mouth.

∎ **FIGURE 2.2 Bryce alone on the class meeting rug**

We know the children have been paying attention as writers as well as readers when imagistic language begins to find its way into their own writing. Dane's words help the reader see the flowers of his opening story line "These two flowers were the last of their kind."

One morning when a dense fog beckoned us to come out and experience the world from inside its mysterious mist, imagistic language flowed. Ian wrote, "The fog is the nightkeeper." Madeleine saw "Shadows all around, trapping me." Alice described "A big gray blanket covering the earth. Grass fading away." Kevin created this playful image: "A water tower head peeking at people's houses." And Ben conveyed a sense of astonishment:

Fog makes roads look like a forest
but when I get near
it disappears.
It must have stepped out of my way!

Organizing much of our reading around genre studies is another way we encourage our students to read as writers. We find it an especially effective way to help developing readers understand that words are the way into the message, not an end in themselves. They begin to see that the format and style used by a writer can shape the way that writer's message is perceived. When our students immerse themselves in the genre of fairy tales, for example, they begin to internalize both the form and structure of the language, and we find it showing up in their writing. Consider some of these beginning sentences that appeared after we had completed our study of fairy tales:

once upon a tuym a grl wus frulikyn in hr yard wen she sa a leprkun.

Once upon a time a girl was frolicking in her yard when she saw a leprechaun.

Madeleine, age six

Wants a panatam thara was a gril thats its nam is Emily and Emily livd in the fouret and shewas a joefl Kid

Once upon a time there was a girl that its name is Emily and Emily lived in the forest and she was a joyful kid.

Emily, age six

Our story begins on a Auttum day.

Jordan, age seven

> I tic Ni EiE OOF THE LAILaCN AND HE WAS GON
>
> I took my eye off the leprechaun and he was gone.
>
> *Marshall, age six*

Emily's story really captures it all:

> Onca open a time thar was a mene old lady and she was so mene to
> avrebody and one day she was not ther. She was magic som times
> She was Vary hlap Flae no body noa hre name and so avry bedy
> clad hre she and she ran in the woods and then she trned in to a nais
> cand wold lady and then avry bady noa hre name.
>
> Once upon a time there was a mean old lady and she was so mean
> to everybody and one day she was not there. She was magic. Some-
> times she was very helpful. Nobody knew her name and so every-
> body called her she and she ran in the woods and then she turned
> into a nice kind old lady and then everybody knew her name.
>
> *Emily, age six*

All the elements of the fairy tale form are there in her story: the requisite "once upon a time," the use of magic (especially in the woods), the fear of things we cannot name, and the happy ending where good clearly prevails.

Sometimes the children's attempts to model a genre lead to wonderfully humorous moments. Jayesh, a child with a gift for words, was writing an adventure/fairy tale modeled after *Raiders of the Lost Ark*. It was a creative story full of the exciting language, challenges, and escapes inherent in the genre. The centerpiece of his story was a scepter that had mysterious powers which he described in the following way:

> The sceptre was made in the 1400s.
> It was first owned by King Samesh.
> Standing 5 feet tall the sceptre was 3 inches wide.
> On top was a big red ruby with little diamonds around it.
> It could heal sick people,
> see into the future,
> and it could mak furniture.
>
> *Jayesh, age seven*

A little confused about the last line, Kathy commented that she understood the first two powers (heal the sick and see into the future) but that she was a little baffled by his third choice (make furniture). Jayesh's response was a classic in seven-year-old logic. "Well," he explained with an absolutely straight face, "you see, I know that in fairy tales things always happen in threes, and making furniture was all I could think of for the third thing!"

Near misses notwithstanding, "messing about" in a genre such as fairy tales prepares our students for the format of the opera stories that become a major focus later in the year.

As rich and varied as opportunities are for exploring the written and spoken word, they represent only one facet of our kaleidoscopic definition of language. We argue that the definition of language is far more complex, and that expressing one's ideas and communicating one's understanding of the world employs many other sign systems such as music, dance, poetry, and the visual arts. It is not so much a language-rich environment as a languages-rich environment that we are striving to construct for our students.

Integrating Music into the Daily Curriculum

Music is a thread woven throughout the fabric of our curriculum. It frames our day, enhances our understanding of story, helps children feel the rhythms of language and math patterns, encourages them to explore the relationship of their bodies to the space around them, makes our voices sing, our bodies dance, and renews our spirits. In the same way that we strive to build a language-rich environment by surrounding our students with literature full of words that roll around on their tongues, so too, do we attempt to immerse them in a musical environment that offers a broad palette of sounds, rhythms, and styles that delight the ear and entice the body to move. Classical, jazz, blues, ragtime, folk, rock—all of it is part of a kaleidoscope of possibilities for exploring feelings and ideas. Music enhances our thinking, feeds our imaginations, and opens doors to fascinating ways of communicating our ideas.

Music frames our day. In our district the buses arrive on a staggered schedule so students arrive in small groups over a fifteen- to twenty-minute period each morning. It is a time for quiet reading alone or with a friend, a chance for us to spend a few moments with a child to hear about the latest important happening (a new baby cousin, a lost tooth), a pause to gather our wits about us and settle in as a community. Because we know the power of music, it is always a part of those first moments of the day. It might be Mozart or Miles Davis, Pete Seeger or Pyotr Tchaikovsky, but it is there, providing a melodic beginning. As the children come to the class meeting rug from all parts of the room their voices get softer and softer until the only sounds left are the soft strains of music playing in the background. It is, to say the least, a most satisfying way to begin the day.

Music is such an integral part of our classroom, first and foremost, because it touches something deep inside us. Like everything else in life, learning moves to a rhythm. "Rhythm," writes Langston Hughes in *The Book of Rhythms,* "is something we share in common, you and I, with all the plants and animals and people in the world, and with the stars and moon and sun, and all the whole vast wonderful universe beyond this wonderful earth which is our home" (1995, 49). Finding that rhythm and learning to move in harmony with it enhances our lives.

Often when we put on a piece of music it is with the intention of simply enjoying its power to elicit our response. Music puts us in touch with the fact that we are made up of many different moods and feelings, and it allows our bodies to validate those feelings. Jazz and ragtime make our hips sway and our feet tap, the Overture from *Coppelia* entices us into a waltz, and a cakewalk compels us to strut our stuff! It can be a tension reliever for antsy bodies and a balm when things are not going well. Problems with a particular child often begin to fade when we take that child's hand and move with him in dance.

But we also have found that music is a powerful teaching tool. We use music to help children translate ideas from one symbol system to another, and often the whole experience is part of a celebration.

To celebrate the first day of fall we play the *Autumn* Movement from Vivaldi's *The Four Seasons,* asking the children to do a quick sketch of what the music suggests. When they bring their sketches to the group to share we are always delighted by the creativity and inventiveness of their interpretations of Vivaldi's music.

Martin's animated sketch is a reflection both of his knowledge of the natural world and his critical listening of the piece (see Figure 2.3).

As he explained his sketch he talked of birds getting ready to fly south, animals gathering food or burrowing beneath the ground to ready themselves for winter, and leaves dropping from trees. The swirly line that runs through the picture, he explained, is the wind he heard in the swirling parts of the music.

Anna Claire's sketch is quite a different autumn scene (see Figure 2.4).

She draws a harvest dance complete with haystacks and jack-o'-lanterns. Her written comment, "This piece I thought was my favorite because I did exactly the vision I had" speaks volumes about the value of using the arts to interpret thinking.

∎ **FIGURE 2.3 Martin's sketch of nature getting ready for winter**

Araka, a first-year student who had been identified as "at risk," responded to the music with a poem:

> Dancing leaves,
> the leaves are twisting
> slow with the music.
> The leaves feel sad.

Reading this poem, we are reminded of why Howard Gardner and Susan Stires choose to look at such children as being not "at risk" but "at promise." Writing her thoughts down was still a major obstacle for Araka (she dictated

■ **FIGURE 2.4** Anna Claire's autumn scene

the poem), but she certainly had the words to convey her feelings, and the music freed her enough to do so.

As we listen to the children talk, it is clear from their comments that they are developing critical listening skills, as well as learning to move between one domain and another. Once our group share is finished the children decide whether they want to do a more complete drawing, or translate the image yet again into the domain of written language, such as a poem, or into that of dance with a movement piece. By offering the children the choice of several sign systems to show their understanding of this piece of music, we hope to create an environment in which each child can find space for his or her preferred mode of learning, as well as offering enticing options that will encourage exploration of new areas. In her book *Can I Play You My Song?*

Rena Upitis (1992) makes the following observation: "Children have a remarkable ability to move in and out of various systems, and by doing so, they learn more about all of the systems they encounter and invent"(54). Our experience has shown that the more opportunities our students have to view the learning experience through multiple lenses, the more they discover about their own talents and strengths. It is especially important to expose young children to a variety of symbol systems for making meaning so they can explore varied paths, benefiting from the richness of a palette so broad that their preferred style of learning is bound to hold a valued place.

Music and movement
As we observe our students we have come to realize that music, like reading, is a transaction between music and listener. The listener interacts with the music, letting it get deep inside while, at the same time, getting deep inside the music. It's a real give and take process. During movement children learn to listen intently, to work with the rhythms, and to follow the music wherever it leads them. The rhythm and beat dictate much of what they do, but their moods also shape their response. We've seen children respond quite differently on different days to the same piece of music. The parallel between music and reading as transactional processes is important to us as teachers of young children because we believe that the more entrees we provide into the world of communication, the more our students view themselves as active participants in the process and the greater their chances of success.

Movement is a natural domain within which young children can think about this idea of making meaning, and it offers tremendous benefits for all types of students. Tense, perfectionist students benefit from the open-ended nature of movement exercises. These are children who, perhaps afraid that they won't get it "right," are very unsure of how to use their bodies in space. Their first attempts at movement are often tight motions in equally tight spaces, but repeated experiences with the improvisational nature of movement gradually help them to loosen up and explore their relationship to the space around them. The importance of such breakthroughs is not lost on us when we realize that learning can't move forward until students, even bright students, are willing to take risks.

We also have discovered that active (and often hyperactive) students thrive in this environment of sanctioned moving about. For some it is mainly an outlet for excess energy, but for others it is a recognition that they need to use their bodies to express themselves in ways they find satisfying. One of the most indelible pictures we hold is of Andrew, a child who often found it very difficult to concentrate, planting himself right in front of the speakers whenever we had movement, mesmerized by the rhythms, wanting to be sure he heard every note. Another is of a group of sports-loving boys who were finding it extremely difficult to write about their love of sports but when we put on some slow, bluesy music and suggested that they mime a baseball game in slow motion, their bodies became a study in fluid interpretation.

All students benefit as they learn to work *with* a piece of music instead of trying to dominate it. As they move, a silent conversation develops between child and music. Their bodies appear to move instinctively, but later discussions reveal that the movement was often shaped by conscious decisions based on critical listening. An excerpt from a discussion we had after the children had had an opportunity to choreograph movement to "In the Hall of the Mountain King" by Edvard Grieg is a good illustration:

Teacher: Tell me about the creeping movement at the beginning of your piece.
Daniel: Well, the music, when it goes Da-da-da-da-da-da-dum, da-da-dum, da-da-dum, makes me think of goblins sneaking up behind someone, so I did these tiny steps on my tiptoes.
Teacher: The same notes were being played near the end of the piece, yet you weren't creeping any longer.
Daniel: Yeah, but at the end the instruments were all loud and playing really fast, so they told me to twirl round and round really fast.

These kinds of comments help us see that while our students are benefiting from the opportunities of expressing their ideas through dance, they are also building critical listening skills and developing the ability to think reflectively about their work, skills which spill over into other areas of their learning. It is important to emphasize that the previous discussion took place *after* the children had time to choreograph the movement. We didn't discuss possibilities or intellectualize beforehand. We gave the children time to "mess about" with movement and music, time to let the music get inside them.

Music and math
Perhaps the greatest benefit of making music such an integral part of teaching is its versatility. There are many times, for example, that we use music in specific ways to build understanding of a mathematical concept such as repetitive patterns. We use this as an example because we think most readers would agree that an understanding of pattern is vital to a child's success as a learner. Pat-

terns are everywhere: in math, science, language, art, music, and dance. If a child doesn't grasp the idea of the predictability of patterns, then each example she meets represents a new challenge. Such a child might see /and/band/sand/ as three completely different words she must learn to spell; she might see 3+1/4+1/5+1 as three separate problems to tackle. The entire learning situation becomes an overwhelming task. Helping children develop an understanding of pattern takes many exposures to many and varied experiences. When working with math concepts, for example, young children benefit not only from hands-on experiences, but also from experiences involving their entire bodies. Music helps children develop understanding of pattern literally from the inside out.

We often begin talking about simple, repetitive patterns, for example, by having the children use manipulatives such as pattern blocks, Multi-links, or Cuisenaire rods to create a two-color sequential pattern. Then we ask them to translate those patterns to body movement. The simplest illustration might be red/blue, red/blue, red/blue becoming stamp/clap, stamp/clap, stamp/clap. Next we ask them to record their patterns using alphabet letters. Again, the simplest might be AB, AB, AB. Then we gather the children and have them listen to a piece of music that has an obvious repetitive pattern. A particularly good example is the Third Movement of Beethoven's Seventh Symphony, which has two distinctly different repeating patterns. We listen for the sprightly A pattern followed by the slow, sustained B pattern, letting our ears become attuned to the points where the patterns change from one to the other. Finally, we divide the class into an A group and a B group, with the direction that as they listen to the Third Movement again, they are to dance only when they hear *their* pattern in the music. We should add that whenever we are involved in a movement exercise one of the ground rules is no voices; all communication must be done through movement alone. It's a practice that goes a long way toward helping children develop focusing skills. (It also does wonders for transition times during the day.)

But children need no reminders to get quiet and focus on the music. Listening intently, bodies ready as they anticipate the end of one pattern and the beginning of the next, they are learning about repetitive pattern from within, their understanding of the concept showing in their movements.

Music and science
Not only math concepts are enhanced by music and movement; science concepts that seem quite abstract suddenly become much clearer when children use their bodies to work toward developing understanding. A lesson on photosynthesis is a good case in point. Pictures, diagrams, experiments, and demonstrations were

valuable aids in helping children move toward an understanding of this phenomenon during our directed lessons, but their grasp of the idea seemed tenuous at best. We don't expect mastery of such concepts at our level, but we did know that a combination of science, music, and movement might make the information more accessible and understandable to our young students.

We often propose the following problem: The class is broken up into groups of five or six. Half the groups are presented the challenge of creating a movement piece demonstrating a leaf at work taking in carbon dioxide and nutrients, manufacturing oxygen, and sending the oxygen out into the atmosphere. The other groups are to create a piece demonstrating a leaf shutting down for the winter. Water and food are no longer able to travel through it, its pigment dries up, and ultimately it desiccates and dies. To underscore their thinking and to frame their movement, the groups work to the *Spring* and *Autumn* Movements, respectively, of Vivaldi's *The Four Seasons*. Our only instruction to the groups is a reminder that, while they could use their voices to plan their piece, the performance must be movement only, choreographed in such a way that the audience would be able to interpret their wordless story.

As the groups go off to different parts of the room to begin solving their problem we move about observing what the children have internalized about the science concepts involved, sometimes offering a comment that helps a stalled group get back on track. The time in which the groups work on their movement pieces is also an excellent opportunity to assess progress in the children's use of collaborative skills. This type of ongoing assessment is valuable to us in our planning for individual children, so this is one of many spaces in the day we design for what Yetta Goodman calls "kid-watching."

These group projects are not meant to be polished performances. The emphasis is very much on process, on the interpretation of the science concept involved. Each group has about twenty minutes to work through their movement problem, after which we meet to share ideas. After each demonstration the audience is asked to reflect on the piece by telling the group three things that worked well and one thing that could make the piece even better. Typical comments might be:

> I like the way nobody told anybody else what to do.

> I could really tell the oxygen was leaving the leaf because Leo ran out of the circle.

> It was hard to tell that the pigment was gone because they were still standing up.

Such critiquing is a simple process, but it reinforces a protocol for talking about student work that we expect students to use in all areas of the curriculum. It is a method we use to help our young students understand that criticism is not always negative, and that a true learning community can be trusted to make the kinds of comments that will clarify and advance our thinking and improve our work.

Mirroring

Development of focusing skills is a wonderful side benefit of using music to teach math and science concepts, but it is one of our primary purposes when we involve our students in a mirroring activity. The whole point of mirroring is to help our students learn to focus their concentration, and music plays a crucial role.

In a mirroring activity the child works with a partner in complete silence, listening to the music and imitating the partner's movements as though looking in a mirror. The initial activity is slow and easy, with children sitting cross-legged, knee-to-knee, palms almost touching, eyes glued to each other. One partner is designated leader and the other partner's job is to follow the leader's movements. The music is kept very slow and repetitive so that the children have time to get used to the idea of following someone when there are no verbal directions (no easy task the first few times). Pachelbel's Canon in D is excellent for first attempts. As the children gain experience with mirroring, we use more complex music and our students experiment with changing position levels from sitting to kneeling to standing.

Once again, although the main idea of the activity is to develop focusing skills, there is always the not-so-secondary purpose of encouraging creative interpretation through movement. Some of our students who struggle to communicate with words show themselves to be eloquent when they communicate through dance. Movement opportunities help us look at those children with fresh eyes, seeing them as successful students who are offering us insights into their learning styles.

These days when teaching time seems to be getting shorter and mandates make courses of study longer, it is astonishing to think about the number of skills being addressed during a simple movement activity. Listening and focusing skills, collaborative skills, creative interpretation, nonverbal communication, and problem solving skills are involved each time this combination of music and movement takes place. It is an extremely valuable and efficient use of time, and the benefits spill over into the rest of the curriculum. As the year progresses, our students listen to each other more closely during class discussions; they focus more intently during group lessons, work more successfully in collaborative teams, and develop more creative ways to solve problems. It is one more example of transferring learning from one domain to another, and it provides one more possibility for making sense of the world.

Pairing Music and Books

A well-written story can stand on its own, but combining a beautiful story with just the right piece of music can make the listening experience magical. We are always searching for books and music that enjoyed separately, would enhance the children's learning, but that taken together, create an all-enveloping experience that is more than the sum of its parts, an experience that transports us to a completely different level of appreciation. For example, when we do a focused study of the environment we are always searching for books that will help our students develop a respect for and sense of awe about the natural world. We want them to internalize the idea that we are inextricably linked with nature, and that, properly cared for, natural treasures both large and small renew and refresh our spirit. We want to expose students to books that evoke feelings of respect for something larger than ourselves.

Uri Shulevitz's *Dawn* is a deceptively simple story of a young child and his grandfather waking up in the predawn and setting out in a rowboat on a misty lake. The story, illustrated with delicate watercolors and told with only one or two words on a page, is mysterious and mesmerizing. The spare text and dreamy illustrations captivate the listener with the power of their simplicity. The pairing of this story with the *Sunrise* Movement from Grofé's *Grand Canyon Suite* sets the stage for a memorable moment.

The movement opens with strings hovering quietly as the characters wake in the gray dawn, flutes suggesting the first notes of birdsong. The music glides as the boy and the grandfather row slowly out onto the misty lake, building in intensity as the morning light brightens on each page, until the glorious crescendo of the final phrases matches the breathtaking full sunrise on the last page of the book. The children's reaction is unforgettable. They sit so entranced by the experience that they almost forget to breathe. When the last word and note die away there is a collective sigh, an acknowledgment that we have shared something special.

From an aesthetic standpoint the experience speaks for itself, but there are pedagogical issues also being addressed by such pairings of books and music: Combining several sign systems seems to make the transaction between child and learning experience more complete. Words and music work together to help children focus and use listening skills more effectively. When we talk with our students after such a reading experience we are always astonished by the perceptive connections children make between story and music.

In reflecting upon *Dawn*, Daniel commented, "I pictured and heard a bird singing at dawn and then it flew away. The sun was boasting about how beautiful she was."

Kevin, whose thoughts ran along the same lines, said, "when the music gets loud the flower is celebrating because it has finally bloomed!"

Adam added this image: "When the flute was playing it sounded like the dew was dripping through the grass."

Mary Kate began her story, "As the darkness fades down. . ."

Araka, who at this point in the year had moved from dictating to using functional spelling, once again turns to poetic language:

> Dawa IS Hape
> The Sn IS Riseg
>
> Dawn is happy
> The sun is rising

Clearly this experience offered wonderful opportunities for our students to build language skills as they listened to each other search for just the perfect word to express an image.

Music also reaches places deep inside us, and this particular combination of book and music provides a tranquil island of time in the children's often hectic lives. Moved by their perceptive interpretations, we suggested that the children take the images they had created inside their heads and get them down on paper. The artist Georgia O'Keeffe was able to "let her brush paint melodies. She let her eye see sound" ("New Mexico Music" by Monica Kulling). We wanted our children to see sound, to capture the music of the sunrise with their art and poetry. Here are a few examples of what they came up with, quickly, right at the moment, beginning with Anna, who sketched animals on their hind legs, dancing and prancing, jumping higher and higher as the sun rose (see Figure 2.5).

Diana's verbal image, fostered by a memory of a video production of the opera *Hansel and Gretel* seen the previous year as part of our opera workshop, conveys the tranquillity of the moment: "Angels come down golden stairs from heaven. They spread their beauty down on the world."

Sometimes the combination of book and music reaches down and sets children's souls dancing. Such is the case when we pair *Charlie Parker Played*

■ **FIGURE 2.5** Anna's animals dancing and prancing

Bebop by Chris Raschka with "Night In Tunisia," a signature song of Charlie Parker's. Chris Raschka has said that he had "Night In Tunisia" in mind when he wrote the book, a fact that seems evident when you hear how the jazzy rhythms frame this story with a captivating beat that has bodies swaying, fingers snapping, and faces grinning in no time. How captivating a beat became clear when Zack's dad reported the following conversation that took place after school the day we read the book. Coming upon Zack searching through the CDs, David asked what he was looking for. Zack's response was, "I can't remember the guy who plays it but I'm looking for that jazzy music that goes, Da-da-da-daaaaa, da-da-da-da, Da-da-da-daaaaa, da-da-da-da, Da-da-da-daaaaa, da-da-da-da. . . . Never leave your cat alone." Zack captured the essence of the piece so perfectly that David immediately reached for "Night In Tunisia"!

A Place for the Unexpected

When we think about creating a learning environment for our students we are reminded of Donald Murray's advice to "expect the unexpected." Contradictory though it may sound, constructing an environment that leaves space for welcoming the unexpected and for exploring the rhythms of learning takes a goodly amount of planning, effort, and background work. It also requires the courage to pay attention to your instincts as well as the ability to let go and trust what children know. But when it all comes together it can be extremely rewarding. We'd like to end this chapter with a tale of such a time. As our children often say, "Our story begins . . ."

Our story began innocently enough when we were browsing in a bookstore one afternoon—hardly surprising since we spend half our lives wandering through bookstores! While contentedly sampling all the new offerings in children's books we came upon a book by Ken Robbins called *A Flower Grows*. The cover was an exquisitely detailed watercolor of an amaryllis in full flower; inside was an equally detailed rendering of an amaryllis bulb, its ungainly appearance giving not even a hint of the secret contained. The juxtaposition of the paintings was arresting, but it was the first sentence in the book that really grabbed us: "Sometimes beauty comes from the most unexpected places." The larger implications of such a statement were not lost on us. The book had to be ours. It wouldn't be the first time we helped our students learn one thing by way of learning something else. We decided on the spot to begin an amaryllis growing experiment, unaware of just how much we all would be changed in the process.

The experiment began in a low-key manner one Monday in late October. We placed an amaryllis bulb on a table next to a blank recording book and a sign that said, "Does anyone know what this is? Write your thoughts in the recording book." The only clue we gave the children was that the bulb would grow into a plant much larger than the bulb itself. Used to dealing with such questions, they immediately began discussing possibilities, many of which gave rise to some very interesting conversation. A lot of good science talk went on that week as the children speculated about the plant that would grow from this bulb. They contemplated possibilities during the school day and continued their musings at home, quizzing their parents to find out what they knew about bulbs and blossoms.

Jeffrey's sketch (see Figure 2.6) is an excellent example of the way some students use drawing to help them think about questions. Looking at Jeffrey's work often reminds us of how important it is to make places in our curriculum

❚ **FIGURE 2.6 Jeffrey's sketch of amaryllis bulb**

for sketching. A child with a severe hearing impairment, Jeffrey is a very analytical student who has taught himself to observe in a completely focused way. This type of scientific sketching, which doesn't involve hearing, allows him to work from his strengths to show what he understands.

By Friday no one had guessed the name of the bulb, so we took out Ken Robbins' book to share with the class. They were fascinated by the pictures of the stately stalk growing with what appeared to be great speed. The tension of seeing the bud get fuller and fuller on each successive page, just a hint of dusty rose color visible through a faint crack in the green cover, kept their attention glued to the book. When we finally turned to the page that revealed the amaryllis in full blossom, "oohs and ahhs" replaced the hush that had fallen over the room.

Young children, as anyone knows who works with them, are full of wonder. They haven't yet developed the veneer of sophistication that keeps them from allowing their sense of wonder to shine through. When our students spied the pot and the soil set up at the work table, they erupted in cheers! It had been one thing to experience the glory of this beautiful flower vicariously; witnessing the marvel firsthand promised to be truly memorable.

Our project, which began with the planting of the bulb on November 5th, was a real lesson in patience because it was a good two weeks before anything happened. Each morning children would head for the window to see if the first green shoot had appeared. Their disappointed faces called to mind the old saying about "watched pots," but their patience was rewarded on November 16th when we were presented with a shoot that measured a full two centimeters. From that point on the task of measuring and recording the growth of the stalk became a coveted job on our weekly job chart.

Over the next few weeks we found that while it may take an amaryllis some time to get going, once the growth begins there seems to be no stopping it. The children were delighted with the speed of the stalk shooting straight upward, and they were very conscientious about following instructions to give the plant a quarter turn each day so that it would continue to grow straight.

Each morning we would record the growth of the stalk in centimeters and inches, marveling at how quickly things were happening. There were some wonderful mathematical understandings developing: As we compared the two measuring charts it was easy for the children to understand that centimeters are smaller than inches because they could see how many more centimeters it took to equal the growth in inches. It was exciting to observe the interest with which different children would go over to measure the stalk at different points in the day, often giving each other minilessons in the necessity of always measuring from the same point, beginning at the end of the ruler, or helping each other decide which was the inches and which was the centimeter side to the ruler.

Our sense of wonder and anticipation grew right along with our plant. What color would the blossom be? When would the second stalk they had discovered begin to bud? How many blossoms would it have? We knew by then that the first stalk would have four.

Finally, on December 9th, one intriguing mystery was solved when the casings had cracked enough to reveal a soft, dusty rose color. The excitement that day was almost palpable. Several children had been sketching growth phases in their science sketchbooks all along, but at our opening meeting on the day the first color became visible through the crack in the bud, it was a unanimous decision that we all had to capture the special moment.

Since we hadn't yet turned off the morning music the lilting strains of Mozart's Clarinet Concerto could still be heard as we gathered our science sketchbooks and settled in around the plant. Conversation came to a complete halt as we tried to capture the life of a bud about to burst into blossom, our mood and senses heightened as the concerto moved into the exquisite Adagio Movement. Struck by the tranquillity of the scene, we realized that once again art and music had made possible one of those priceless moments of shared experience in our classroom community.

By December 11th the casings on two of the buds were ready to burst, a reality that caused no small amount of concern because it happened to be a Friday and the children were absolutely certain that the buds would blossom over the weekend and no one would be present to witness the event. The only way we could allay their anxieties was for Kathy to promise to take the plant home over the weekend so she, at least, could witness the event and report every detail on Monday.

Enormous blossoms did, in fact, greet her Sunday morning as she walked into her family room and, as she reported to the rest of us, their beauty almost took her breath away!

The wait until the children arrived Monday morning seemed endless. The amaryllis sat in a place of honor on the windowsill directly opposite the entrance to the room so that it would be the first thing the children saw as they entered the room. Early morning light filtered through the enormous petals, spreading a diffuse rosy light.

The first child to come through the doorway stopped dead in his tracks and simply stood, awestruck by the sight of such grandeur. Then he raced into the hall, found another child and, still without saying a word, pulled her into the doorway. The two of them stood in silent wonder, understanding intuitively that words would have been intrusive. For those of us who worry that a sense of awe and wonder is missing from the lives of too many children, it was a moment to savor.

And it was a moment that would be repeated over and over as each new child was brought to the doorway. First they stopped and stared, then they walked right up to the blossoms, examining the petals closely, feeling the velvety softness, observing the way the light filtered through the petals. Some of the children grabbed paper and pencil and began sketching the amaryllis in great detail, trying to capture every nuance of the blossoms. It was almost as though the children needed time to absorb the beauty of this flower before they could even begin to find words to talk about it.

But when the talk began at our joint morning meeting, the words flowed nonstop. It started with Steffi's wistful comment: "I wish my dad could be here. It's his birthday and seeing the amaryllis would be a wonderful birthday present."

Someone suggested she write a poem about it to share with him. Someone else suggested we write a class poem . . . and we were off. For the next fifteen minutes the schedule was set aside while we brainstormed ideas, trying to capture in words what we felt when we looked at this beautiful flower. The awe we were all feeling was reflected in many of the comments:

> Awesome!
> Cool, man!
> Gorgeous!

Some comments were the result of close observation:

> Velvety!
> The stamens look like they are asking us to come in.
> Pretty
> Smooth
> Big
> Shooting up
> Look at those hot pink petals!

Others were statements of absolute wonder:

> Wow, this can't be happening!
> It finally blossomed!

When everyone had an opportunity to let the words spill out, we began to look at our brainstorming list so that we could choose just the right words to capture the essence of our experience. (The thought occurred to us later that the shared experience of a class poem was the perfect response to the shared experience of living with this project for several months. Writing the poem at that moment felt right, and that seems to be the bottom line of much of the most fruitful learning in our classroom.) As we talked we agreed that some of the words such as "Awesome!" and "Gorgeous!" were perfect as is. Others, such as "Big," were not quite right and needed more work before they conveyed just the right image.

But the poem was already sitting there in the children's words, and with a little rearranging of lines it came to the fore:

Ode to Our Amaryllis
This can't be happening!
Our amaryllis blossomed!
Awesome,
Huge, Hot pink,
Beautiful,
Smooth, curly stamens saying,
"Come in."

It may seem a little pretentious for six- and seven-year-olds to be writing "odes," but these children were adamant about the title. Because we read poetry to them daily they were familiar with many different types of poems and the moods they create. They knew that an ode was a love song, and a love song was exactly what they wanted to write in honor of this magnificent flower.

Excited as they were about the class poem, it was only the beginning for most of the children. Throughout the day we would see small groups of children huddled around the amaryllis sketching and writing.

There is the innocence of the young child's awe in Jackie's opening lines:

Amaryllis, with her petals nice and bright,
She's come to wonder me.

Jordan's love affair with words shines through his images (see Figure 2.7):

The Amaryllis
You shoot up a green sprout.
Then you blossom with delight.
As you lean to the light,
You boast about you!

■ **FIGURE 2.7 Jordan's amaryllis sketch and poem**

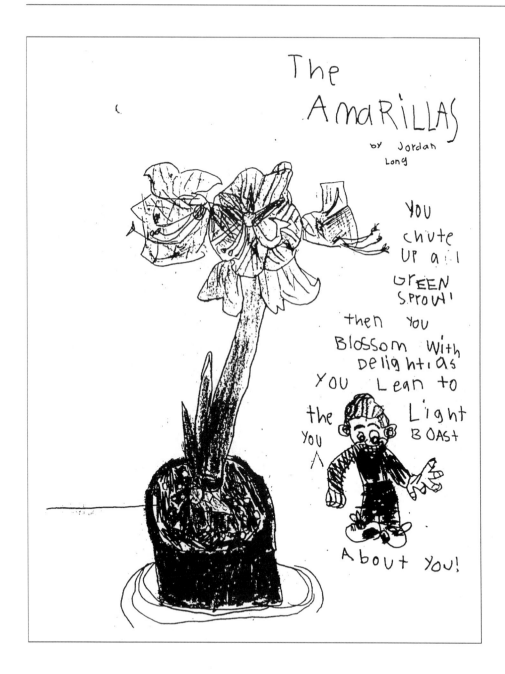

Marvin kept his short and to the point:

> A flower grows that I like,
> And a boy says, 'Cool, man!'

Natael used her artist's eye to capture in words something no one else had seen:

Queen of the Flowers

> The queen of the flowers
> opens up her stunning, soft petals.
> Her lovely, green, sparkling dress
> shines upon you.

The stem as a long, flowing dress, the stateliness of the plant suggesting royalty—how much larger this six-year-old had made this experience for all of us. We had been captivated by the flower's literal beauty, but she had taken us into an entirely different dimension and opened up a whole new realm of possibility.

Her classmates borrowed and expanded upon her metaphor many times during the next few weeks, especially as the first stalk began to wilt and the second stalk began to blossom. What was both startling and moving to us was the implicit understanding these young children had of the natural sequence of the life cycle: Death is a part of life; one life ends and another begins; the old gives way to the new. Daniel's poem is a good example of that understanding:

Amaryllis

> As the Queen of the Flowers withers,
> A new queen is chosen to take her place.

Evan's poem alludes to the fact that we live on in others:

The Drooping Amaryllis

> The drooping amaryllis
> passes away
> as another grows
> like a twin.

Natael, in writing about the second stalk, carried through the idea of royalty in a poem that turned out to be the second in a trilogy:

The Princess

The dead Queen of the Flowers droops
as it falls away.
Her lovely young daughter takes over.
The princess opens up
her stunning, soft petals.
Her lovely, green, sparkling dress
shines upon you.

Clearly this was a child plumbing the depths of her artistic sensibility to respond to this gift of nature. Notice the way she carries through her analogy of mother and daughter, queen and princess; the way she repeats a line from a previous poem. We had not taught specific lessons in such things. Much of her work was a marvel to us, but to her it was as natural as breathing.

The last in the trilogy, written as the second stalk began to wilt, showed a depth of emotion and sensitivity that took our breath away and convinced us that this child's gifts were something to be savored and nurtured. At the time Natael was still very much at a developmental stage in her acquisition of writing skills, but her poem shows a depth of expression that far outstripped her writing development, and her rough draft is a testament to the power of functional spelling when children are trying to communicate:

The Prinsas

The Prinsas
Wepss and Wepss
Staring at The
Dach of Hr Mach
She Grassfoe
Brooss to WeP A Gon.

The Princess II

The princess weeps and weeps
Staring at the death of her mother
She gracefully bows to weep again.

This is a child gifted in art, with the soul of a poet. Our responsibility is to make certain that our classroom is a place where she will feel validated and understood when she uses her remarkable gifts to communicate her understanding of the world.

Experiencing the growth of the amaryllis was nothing short of magical for all of us privileged enough to be a part of it. The miracle of the growth cycle, the anticipation of the appearance of the blossoms, the total absorption in the grandeur of the amaryllis in full bloom, and the response to that grandeur through sketches, poetry, and sheer wonderment forever changed both our learning worlds and our personal worlds. Perhaps most important, it showed that our learning community was most alive when there was very little distinction between those worlds.

Chapter 3

Poetry Immersion

The words of the true poems give you more than poems . . .   —*Walt Whitman*

Poetry was not always such a natural part of our curriculum. When we first started teaching together, we hadn't yet developed an understanding of the power of poetry as a metaphor through which children could communicate their beliefs about what they observe and understand. The process through which we reclaimed poetry as a natural response to our learning, one that has provided our students with a unique lens, has evolved over several years.

It is difficult now for us to imagine a learning circle that isn't wide enough to include poetry as a response. Poetic language had always been part of the everyday speech of our students. Kara, for example, bounced through our classroom door the day after she had started ice skating lessons and announced, "Yesterday was the first day of my new life!" Leo asked after our amaryllis had bloomed, "Amaryllis, why do you know when you should bloom?" Jackie said about the amaryllis, "She's come to wonder me."

The irony was that although our children would dutifully attempt to write poetry when asked, the poetic form was not often a response they chose. One of the questions we had been wrestling with for years was how to create an environment that would allow children's natural poetic response to rise to the surface and flourish. Poetry starters, like "If I were . . ." or "Some-day . . ." just didn't seem to be enough. The poems that the children chose to write during writing workshop were clearly lacking in the kinds of poetic imagery that were showing up in their prose writing. At the same time we were finding phrases like Jayesh's image in his story about birds, "partners dancing right smack in front of the world . . . ," we were finding poems like the unimaginatively titled "My Poem," with phrases like "a pencil is a pencil" or "a book is a book."

We knew these kids had it in them. We just couldn't figure out how to put all the ingredients together, how to help them get to the point where they would understand what Lucille Clifton (1995) means when she talks of poetry coming from her "whole insides," that she didn't choose poetry; it chose her. We didn't know what we needed to do to help these children create in Arnold Adoff's words "the poem singing into your eyes" (1993, 20).

A poetry unit wasn't the answer, either. Highlighting poetry four weeks a year would not help the children discover poetry as a valid response at any time, even at home in the bathtub. We wanted our students to see poetry everywhere, looking at the world with a poet's eye. We wanted them to believe as Naomi Shihab Nye does, that poets do not look at the world the way the world expects them to:

> . . . Nothing was ugly
> just because the world said so. He really
> liked those skunks. So, he reinvented them
> as valentines and they became beautiful.
> (1990)

Tom Romano's class at the New Hampshire Writing Program helped provide some insights. On the first day of class, as we sat in nervous anticipation, Tom explained that his goal was to get poetry back into our bones. To achieve that goal, he read contemporary poetry to us every morning, totally immersing us in the language of Howard Nemerov, Marge Piercy, Anne Sexton, Mekeel McBride, and Paul Janeczko, among others. And as Tom read we noticed several things begin to happen: Our behavior in bookstores changed. No longer did we automatically gravitate toward the children's section of the store. We now found ourselves perusing the poetry shelves, as well, ecstatic when we discovered Anne Sexton's *Transformations* and Marge Piercy's *Stone, Paper, Knife* on the shelf, surprised we were so disappointed when William Stafford's *Things That Happen Where There Aren't Any People* was nowhere to be found.

Our conversations in the evening more often revolved around poetry. One night a discussion of Bruce Weigl's haunting images in *Song of Napalm* kept us up until two o'clock in the morning. Other nights found us running back and forth between rooms in the dorm to share new poems we had discovered or arresting images we had noticed.

The biggest change though, had to do with writing poetry. Neither of us had written poetry since high school. Tom never required that we write poetry. He just kept reading poems every morning and offering writing opportunities. One night, Kathy awakened knowing she had to give voice to memories of her father she had carried around for years.

Love Song

Soft flannel caressing my cheek,
I press my ear close against my father's chest
His heartbeat
A reassuring mantra of security.
Breathing deeply,
I inhale comforting aromas . . .
Old Spice, tobacco, Lifebouy soap . . .
Plain, honest
Smells of my father.

Precious morning moments
The four-year-old
Too young for school,
The steelworker father
Between night turn and sleep.

Side by side we lay,
The warm, familiar chair enveloping us
In our private world,
And my father begins to sing
Melancholy strains of Ol' Man River,
His deep, rumbling voice
Vibrates through my being
Surrounding me with his love.

A trip down a country road shortly after arriving in New Hampshire prompted
Sharon to write a poem:

Getting Older

The sign on the road says
Slow Duck
Crossing,
And I wonder about this new kind of duck.
And I wait for these
slow New Hampshire ducks
to waddle across the road,
imagining *Make Way for Ducklings*
right here in Portsmouth.
It's only a short beat of time before I realize,

> that the only slow duck I will see
>
> is in my mind;
>
> synapses not quite touching.

Without consciously thinking about it, poetry *had* become imbedded in our bones.

By immersing us in poetry, Tom also helped us realize how important it is to hear poetry read aloud. Ashley Bryan, whose oral reading of poems seems to reinvent them, believes that poetry, like music, must be heard. For him, not hearing a poem read aloud is "In many ways . . . like a musician never hearing songs sung but learning to love them only from sight reading the music" (in Copeland and Copeland 1994, 74).

We learned that listening to a poem once was never enough. By the time we began to absorb what the poem was saying to us, Tom would have finished reading. Eve Merriam, in an interview said, "children should be encouraged to read the poems at least twice: once to get the sense, and the second to get the music" (in Copeland 1993, 122).

How did all of our work in New Hampshire translate once we returned to our classroom? Once again we realized that it was the changes and insights into our own learning that enlarged and shaped our classroom curriculum in new ways. The answer to our dilemma about teaching poetry to children began to emerge. As Tom had helped us to see, immersing children in poetry, reading poetry every day, and giving children the opportunity to write was part of the answer.

Our day now begins with poetry, and not only do we read the poem several times, but we also write many of our favorite poems on big poster boards and display them around the room. The children can see these poems all the time. Hearing the poem, *as we read along,* gives us a better understanding of the poem. It also allows us to see what a poem looks like. By making the poetry so visible, the children notice that poems come in a variety of shapes and sizes. They notice that poetry looks different from stories. We start to see poems that look like Scott's in Figure 3.1.

Remembering our experience in Tom Romano's class, we read and listen to a variety of poetry every day, offering what Eve Merriam calls a "smorgasbord," so that each child can find something to which she can relate (in Copeland 1993, 121). Although we enjoy humor in poetry, we know that funny, rhyming poems are not the only kind of poetry kids enjoy. We read poems from Eloise Greenfield's *Honey, I Love,* revel in shange's *i live in music,* and make selections from

▪ **FIGURE 3.1 Scott's fog poem**

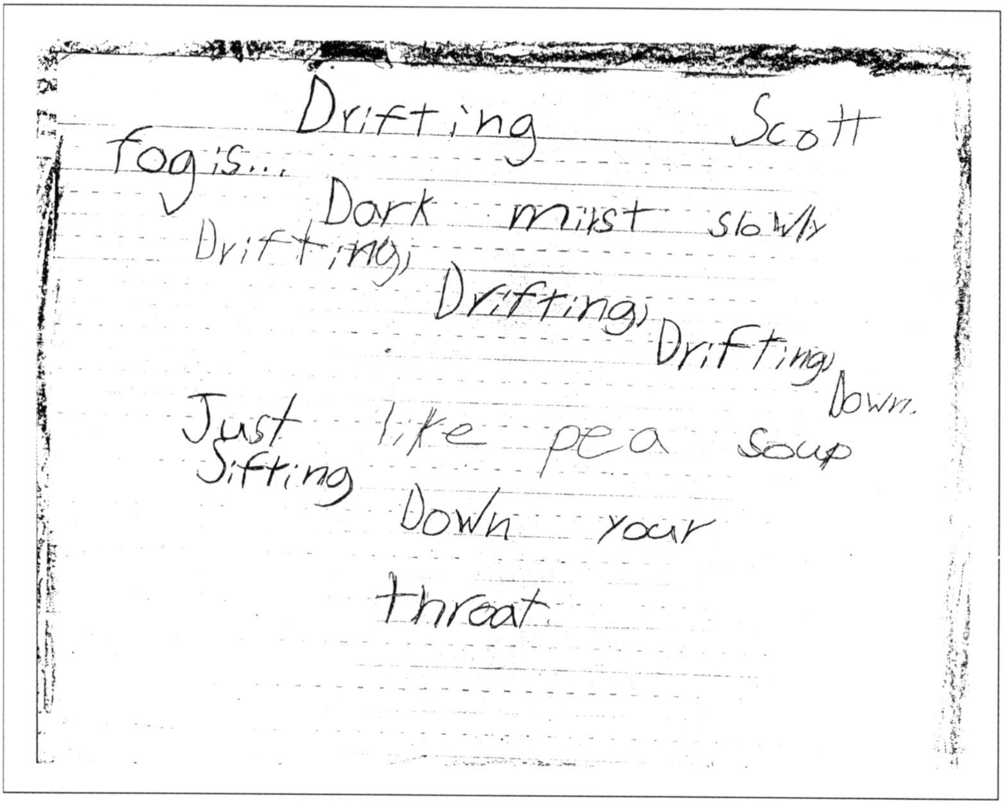

Drifting   Scott
Fog is...
    Dark mist slowly
Drifting,
    Drifting, Drifting,
                   Down.
Just like pea soup
Sifting
    Down your
     throat.

Jack Prelutsky's collection *The Random House Book of Poetry for Children*. Some of the poems we read fit with our focused studies. When we study nutrition, for example, we read lots of food poems. Our kids quote from Bruce Springsteen's version of *Chicken Lips* as we get ready for our class breakfast, thankful that it isn't "mama's soup surprise" we will be serving (in Disney 1991, 38). When we study insects, we read lots of bug poems. Georgia Heard's "Dragonfly" (1992) is a favorite. And while painting poppies in the style of Georgia O'Keeffe, we read from Carl Sandburg's "Crossing Ohio": "Pick me poppies in Ohio, mother. Pick me poppies in a back yard in Ashtabula" (1982, 53).

    Sometimes the poems we read have the power to transform our mood. One rainy November day when our gray northern Ohio skies hung lower than usual, we all felt the need of something to get us going. We began the morning with a reading of Ralph Fletcher's "A Writing Kind of Day" from *Water Planet*. It opens with the lines "It is raining today, a writing kind of day" (1991, 15). Suddenly our perspective changed. With a few well-chosen words Fletcher had transformed a depressing gray day into a cozy invitation, beckoning us to snuggle in and enjoy the unexpected opportunity to let our imaginations roam. Who could resist such an invitation?

Listening to beautiful language filled with poetic images really captures kids' imaginations and makes them reach in their understanding of metaphor. We couldn't wait to share Naomi Shihab Nye's *This Same Sky* after we discovered the book at an NCTE convention. Many of the poems in this book are written on a sophisticated level, but we knew they would appeal to some of our kids. Adam, an advanced second grader, picked up our invitation. He spent several hours one morning immersed in the book, and then sat down to write a poem he called "When the Sun Sets Over the Mountains." It was inspired by Edith Sodergran's "Dawn" and was a spontaneous creation, written in one burst:

When the Sun Sets Over the Mountains

When the sun sets over the mountains
the clouds join together
and the tiniest drop of water falls
from heaven.
Then another and another.
Lightning flashes, thunder rumbles
and even snow dances down.
Then the sun rises
and the snow filled mountains
sing their song.

Adam

Adam used "Dawn" as a stepping-off place for his poetry. Then he made the poem his own. "Morning rises red out of the ocean," in Adam's hands, became "then the sun rises and the snow filled mountains sing their song."

Arnold Adoff's *Eats* is another book that grabs kids right away. We still hold onto a vivid picture of Eric, a beginning reader, sitting on the class meeting rug, tightly holding on to *Eats*. At first, he would ask us to read and reread "The Apple." Eventually, he started reading the poem on his own. Eric read that poem so many times that six years later, *Eats* automatically opens to that spot. His smudgy fingerprints still adorn the page. They are a reminder to us that poetry can be the key that unlocks the reading process. When Eric could read "The Apple," his ability to read other books soared. He realized that words come together to convey ideas. With that new understanding a part of him, Eric was able to return to James Marshall's *Three by the Sea* with renewed confidence and was soon losing himself in the humor of those zany stories.

The centrality of poetry in our curriculum is underscored by the fact that each child has his own poetry folder. Every time he hears or reads a poem he especially likes, he can make a copy for the poetry folder. Original poetry also belongs there. The children can read the folders whenever they want. During Sustained Quiet Uninterrupted Reading Time (SQUIRT), many children pull out the folders and reread old favorites. Kara would sprawl on the loft surrounded by her poetry, reading and sorting. The favorite poem of the moment would end up on the top of the pile. She would often ask to take her folder home to share with her family. Without consciously thinking about it, many of the children would memorize these favorite poems. Around the classroom, or at recess, we would catch wisps of poems. As the children swung back and forth on the playground equipment, the air would carry Eloise Greenfield:

> Went to the kitchen
> Lay down on the floor
> Made me a poem
> Still got it
> Still got it
> (from "Things" in *Honey, I Love*)

Or Eve Merriam:

> You can take away my mother
> you can take away my sister,
> but don't take away
> my little transistor.
> (from "Umbilical" in *Poems That Sing to You*)

These poems were part of these children, available whenever they were needed.

Saying the poems aloud becomes more than just a listening experience for our students. Experiencing poetry this way becomes a physical response. As they play with the sounds of words, they give life to the description of reading poetry out loud in James Wright's "Saying Dante Aloud." He writes, "You can feel the muscles and veins rippling in widening and rising circles, like a bird in flight under your tongue" (1990, 267). As our children roll the words around in their mouths, they actually feel their shapes and contours. The "Ga-lunks" in Georgia Heard's "Frog Serenade" from *Creatures of the Earth, Sea, and Sky* ring through our room like true frog calls, sounding more and more authentic as the children play with the sound of the word "Ga-lunk," enjoying the vibration in their throats as they drop their voices lower and lower.

They also enjoy hearing poems that they can then read aloud with friends, and the fun of blending voices with another reader has become a big part of poetry reading in our room. Sometimes that means reading poems actually written for two voices. "The Honeybee" from Paul Fleischman's *Joyful Noise* is a poem read with great gusto by our first and second graders. At other times two children will simply decide to share the reading of a poem they both love. SQUIRT time will often find pairs of children tucked away in corners, practicing a poem they will read later either to the class or on station READ, the school radio station.

One benefit is that our students are gaining skill and confidence in their reading ability. We ask them to follow the steps listed below before reading a poem as a performance:

> Did you practice reading your poem for fluency and expression?
> Did you read your poem to three friends?
> Did you read your poem to a teacher?

This gives them an opportunity to become more fluent in their oral reading. Since they are choosing their own poems, they are highly motivated to work on learning to read them. Expression and attention to punctuation improve because they want to convey the feeling of the poem. Poetry makes a common meeting ground for students at different levels of development. Often a developing reader and a more accomplished reader will be caught by the same poem. The more advanced reader then acts as a mentor for his friend.

Many of our poetry books become covered with yellow Post-it Notes because when one child finds a poem she likes, she puts a Post-it Note on that page to let us know we should read that poem to the whole class. Maria and Mary Kate found six poems about snow that we absolutely had to read in Jane Yolen's *Weather Report*. Their Post-it Notes are still visible even after they have moved on to third grade. Kids the following year are delighted to come upon these dog-eared yellow flags signaling choices their friends have made in the past.

Because the language really does enter their bones, many children use similes without consciously thinking about it. We had not discussed simile at all when Nika wrote "The wind hoots like the owl in the night." Melanie's description of "HSLICABTF" or "Leaves slithering around," in her September of first-grade writing, just slithered off her pencil. Slithered was part of her vocabulary. It wouldn't happen if poetry reading, writing, and the close observation it requires were not an integral part of the environment.

Knowledge of poetic forms is also evident in the children's work. When Daniel decided to write an anti-love poem about hot dogs, he had no choice but to call it "Ode to Hot Dogs." He remembered our "Ode to Our Amaryllis." Borrowing from Arnold Adoff's "Inspiration: Chocolate," where the poet wants to "live forever in the flavor of your brown," Daniel used the form of an ode but gave it an unusual twist. He wrote:

Ode to Hot Dogs

Oh, hot dogs
I hate you so,
I wish I could
live in the warmness of hamburgers
instead of you!

Because the language enters their bones, poetic language and visual imagery show up in some unexpected places. As part of a science and math experiment we were conducting about patterns, Anna Claire's Dad brought an ugly looking black box into the room one morning. He explained that this rather uninteresting box was called an oscilloscope and that it would allow us to *see* sound. As the children began to describe what they were seeing on the screen, Sharon recorded the conversation, and when she read back what they had said, we all realized that a poem had quietly taken shape. Our children had taken Naomi Shihab Nye's advice and reinvented that black box once they saw the magic it contained. They had discovered the sleeping poems that were hiding in "the bottoms of our shoes" (1990, 144). They turned an ordinary black box into an extraordinary poem:

Oscilloscope

Oscilloscope
Patterns repeat
Again and again—
Wrinkling up,
Hard rain,

> Sound vibrations
> Dotted lines,
> Repeating mountains,
> Running like lightning.
> Oscilloscope

Poetry Immersion Workshop

Rich environments make for rich experiences. We learned from Tom Romano that poetry immersion was one key to creating such environments. As we saw our children's passion for poetry growing, the idea of an immersion workshop with experts grew. Linda Rief, at the 1995 NCTE convention in San Diego, talked about how important it is for children to study writers they admire. She believes it is necessary for budding writers to try on the style of experts, in order to find their own writers' voice. X. J. Kennedy tells us not to worry about imitating writers we admire: "Eventually you will come to sound not like them anymore, but like yourself." (in Janeczko 1994, 105) The more we thought about the importance of mentors as part of the immersion process, the more we thought about inviting a writer to be a poet-in-residence in our school. What better way to have our children study an expert writer? We also happened to have a poet right in our own backyard. Lynn Powell, the mother of one of our students, was also a poet for the Ohio Arts Council and more than happy to become an artist-in-residence at our school. We, along with several other staff members, wrote a grant to the Ohio Arts Council for a five-week poetry residency.

Lynn's residency helped to focus our attention on poetry. Not only were our students able to use her as a mentor, but we, as teachers, were able to watch a poet go about the business of writing poetry. She spent time in our classroom twice a week working with our students as they wrote. We watched Lynn weave her magic as she seemed to know exactly which questions to ask. A group poem about the moon banally started with "The moon is a crystal ball. The moon is a shining pearl." After Lynn asked *who* would have a crystal ball, and whether someone was wearing the pearl, the poem was transformed.

> The moon is Zeus' crystal ball.
> The moon is a shiny pearl
> the night wears.

Just as working with Tom Romano helped us see what changes we needed to make in the classroom, watching Lynn interact with the children moved us one step closer to finding Adoff's "poem singing into your eyes." She helped *all* of us look at the world from a different perspective, observe closely, think in images, and ask questions that would make our thinking bigger. Because these children were, and are, immersed in poetry and poetic language, that language becomes part of them. Zack, a first grader, wrote a poem about autumn:

Autumn Is . . .
A red red leaf on the ground in the world.
A nut on the ground
with the leaf.
And I, me , see it all.

During a conference about the poem Sharon asked Zack if he meant his last line to say, "I, me, see it all." Perhaps he had meant to say "I see it all." Zack assured her that he had in fact meant "I, me." He said poets say that all the time. He had heard that phrasing before. What amazed us was that this was his first attempt at writing poetry. Yet he was so sure of how a poet writes.

Scott was another child who was sure of poetic language. His original poem looked like this:

Fall Is . . .
Yellow and red leaves drifting away.
Halloween is close.
School is starting.
Homework again.
Oh, no!

During a writing conference Sharon asked Scott about his reference to homework. She was surprised that Scott didn't like it, since he often brought in work from home when it wasn't required. Scott assured her that he did enjoy doing homework. It was just that he thought that kids would expect that line. He had read lots of poems that ended like that. They discussed the fact that his poetry should be true to his feelings. Scott decided he would change the last line of his poem. Here is the revised version.

Fall Is . . .
Yellow and red leaves drifting away.
Halloween is close.
School is starting.
Old friends again.

Asking questions that helped these writers clarify their thinking was a skill we had learned by observing our professional poet at work.

Children began to see possibilities for poems in other writing. Austin, in responding to the *Spring* Movement from Vivaldi's *The Four Seasons,* wrote this detailed description:

> I like when it gose oow.oow.oow. because it sownins like the birds are singing music. In my hed it looks like a butuaful pitcher. With bird swoping down to the butuafull water of the lake. oow.oow. oow. bird birds birds, How I like the birds music.

> I like when it goes ooh, ooh, ooh because it sounds like the birds are singing music. In my head it looks like a beautiful picture with birds swooping down to the beautiful water of the lake. Ooh, ooh, ooh. Birds, birds, birds. How I like the birds' music.

When Austin read his story to Kathy they were both caught by the line "birds swooping down to the beautiful water," and Austin was excited by Kathy's suggestion that this arresting image could be the beginning of a poem. He went to work immediately, and his second draft looked like this:

> Birds swooping down to the beautiful water
> Singing as they pass along
> Some are black
> Some are gray
> Many colors of birds
> Going faster than bats,
> Singing quietly their beaks open and close
> gliding back up to the middle of the sky.

He was well on his way toward developing that one line into a beautifully evocative poem. After a walk in the fog, Emily wrote in her invented spelling:

> Shimary silvr miset the Erath is a jowale
> watr on rakacs are butaful
> a nisa warm blakit of faog
> chidrin makeing made pies
> goldin trees with silvr coding
> warl ice crem with choclit sraup
> flowrs with a gold coding
> crstl's drap from tree's

Draft two (or in her words, *drift two*) kept some of the same images, adding details:

> shimary silvr miset sarod's me
> the erath is a jowale and I am rich
> watre on rakasI sit on are butaful
> a nisa warm colit and pelow I lia on
> gold in tree's with silvr coding
> I wish I watch childin makeing made pies.

When Emily read this draft at her next conference she commented to Kathy that she had used lots of "jewel language." It was the perfect opportunity to talk about the power of metaphor and, as they talked, they numbered all the phrases that contained "jewel language" (the numbered phrases in the draft).

> 1. shimary silvr miset sarod's me
> 2. the erath is a jowale and I am rich
> watre on rakasI sit on are butaful
> a nisa warm colit and pelow I lia on
> 3. gold in tree's with silvr coding
> I wish I watch childin makeing made pies.
> 4. crstl's dropping from tree's.

Rereading what had evolved into a beautifully imagistic poem, Kathy recognized an opportunity to help Emily make her thinking even bigger. What would happen, Kathy asked if you moved the line, "The earth is a jewel and I am rich" to the end of the poem? After reading it that way, Emily's eyes lit up and she said, "Oh, I see. I talk about gold and silver and crystals and then I say "The earth is a jewel and I am rich." By knowing the kind of question to ask, Kathy was able to help Emily see that moving one line made the entire poem come together. This was her final draft:

The Fog
> Shimmery, silver mist surrounds me,
> Golden trees with silver coating,
> Crystals dropping from trees,
> The earth is a jewel,
> And I am rich.

As important as learning what questions to ask was learning when to leave a child alone. Evan decided he needed to write a rhyming poem. His poem was "Winter Splinter."

Winter Splinter

Winter winter cold as a splinter
I wish it were winter every day.
I love May but it will decay
every day of winter.

Evan was quite pleased with his poem. He liked the way it sounded. He especially liked the rhymes and thought winter as a splinter made sense. We talked
about forcing rhymes. We asked him whether his poem said everything he
wanted to say about winter. Evan stayed firm. His poem was "Winter is a
splinter." His repetition of the word winter in the first line showed he was on
the right track. But he would not change one word of his poem. He did explain
to other children about being careful about using rhymes just to use rhymes.
During this time, we wondered what we could do differently to help Evan edit
his poem, convinced that there must be something we were missing. Lynn
assured us that the simple fact was that, at this stage, Evan found it difficult to
set aside a poem he had written. It didn't mean he hadn't learned from the
experience. She suggested we accept his decision, that things would change as
Evan had more opportunities to write. Sure enough, several weeks later, when
he decided to write a poem about the sunset, he wrote, "The sunset is God's
finest silk on the floor." There was not a forced rhyme to be found. Clearly, he
had internalized much of what we had talked about but had needed to feel
ownership of his ideas and to move ahead when he was ready.

Sometimes students get carried away with the idea of drafts and assume that
every poem needs to be reworked. After that walk in the fog, Andreas saw this:

Mysterious mist turns
Black and green into black
Cars disappear and appear
Cloud white curtains.

After rereading his draft, he decided he wasn't satisfied with it. Sharon
thought the images were vivid, but Andreas thought his poem needed more
work. Unlike Evan, he was eager to start on draft two. He wanted to use the
image "cars disappear and appear" as a starting point for another poem.
Andreas then wrote:

Cars play hide and seek
in mysterious mist.
Suddenly mysterious mist

> turns brown and green
>
> into black and white
>
> like an old TV

When he finished writing, Andreas was able to say, "The poem I wrote all evolved from this one line, 'cars disappear and appear.'" He was aware of the process he was using to write his poetry, as well as having the vocabulary to explain in words what he was doing. His second attempt was certainly an evocative poem all on its own. When we looked at the two drafts, though, it was clear that Andreas did not realize how poetic his language had been in his first version. He was enjoying the idea of drafting, using a line from his first draft as the seed for a new poem. He didn't realize that his first draft was in fact a poem. That is the point when the teacher has to step in and say, "Stop! Don't throw those drafts away. You've written two powerful poems. You don't need a third draft." This idea of knowing when to stop was demonstrated concretely one day by potter Chris Breuer, when he was showing us how to make a beautiful pot on a potter's wheel. One minute the pot was growing taller in his deft hands and the next it looked totally misshapen. Chris had worked the pot too long. He said, "You have to know when to stop."

You have to know when to stop when you write poetry, too. As teachers helping children to find authentic ways of responding to the world we have to help them understand that sometimes our first instincts are the best ones. Just because you know how to draft doesn't mean you always have to write a second or third version of a poem. Of course, in Andreas' case he ended up with two equally interesting poems!

The opportunity of working with a professional poet was not only opening up new worlds for our students, it was helping us internalize the kinds of questions and comments one needed to ask to help students uncover the possibilities waiting within their work.

Besides working in the classroom, Lynn had several workshops with teachers that provided uninterrupted time to immerse ourselves in the writing of poetry while working with an expert. Although actual contact hours for the poetry residency added up to five weeks, we were able to stretch the residency over a ten-week period, thus giving teachers time to work with poetry in the classroom and bring questions and examples to the teacher workshops. As we had discovered while taking Tom Romano's course, writing poetry ourselves gave us insights into the writing process. We realized that we had more difficulty writing when Lynn chose the topic. When she said, "Think of a food that carries meaning and then try it as a recipe," the topic was too narrow. The words didn't flow and resulted in papers filled with crossouts and false starts. It helped us see how important it was for children to choose their own topics. Making these workshops a part of the grant allowed time for teachers to become more comfortable with poetry and insured the likelihood that poetry would remain an integral part of the curriculum long after the residency ended.

Lynn invited dancer Nusha Martynuk to spend two days as a visiting artist, working with individual classes, choreographing movement to class poems children had written. Nusha spent the first part of each lesson moving to music with the children. Then she would read the poems and talk with the students about possibilities for using their bodies to express the poetic ideas. It was difficult, at first, for our children to move their bodies without adding their voices. They kept wanting to add sound. Nusha's advice, "Make your whole body listen," helped us to move without using words. Eventually, like Natael, we discovered "A poet is someone who lets her feelings dance." Like the writing of the poetry itself, the expression of feeling through dance gave children the opportunity to reach inside themselves to tap into a response.

Inquiry

The power of poetry to "take us on an adventure" (Leo) and "paint pictures in our minds" (Scott) began to surface through the immersion workshop. The power of poetry to help us think in different ways also began to emerge. Poetry could help us see things from several viewpoints, sometimes in startling ways. Ian helped us see "A poet is someone who can shrink you down to the size of a leaf." We began to discover, along with the poet Deborah Chandra, that "Poetry should make children question and explore events of their lives" (in Copeland and Copeland 1994, 100). When Maria wanted to know "what is the sea?" she asked the question as poetry:

> What is the sea?
> My child I am the tears of the earth. Even the earth cries.

When our children studied insects, they scientifically gathered information. They read books, gazed at sketches, and observed as many bugs as they could. It was through poetry, however, that they reached another level of understanding. In poems, the children were able to interview their insects while using the knowledge they had already gained:

> Walking Leaf,
> Why do you have veins like a leaf?

> Does your disguise keep you safe from the
> holy hands of the praying mantis?
>
> *Class Poem*

Together, the class came up with these images for a walking leaf. In the discussion, Daniel talked about a walking leaf being concerned with praying mantises because he said, "they even eat butterflies!" Anna Claire thought that "holy hands" would work as an image because it was a "praying" mantis after all.

After the class composed this poem, several children decided to try their own versions. Paul was entranced with the walking stick's ability to camouflage himself:

> Walking leaf,
> I wish I was camouflaged like you
> so I could walk anywhere without
> anybody seeing me.

A study of animals resulted in this poem about a wolf:

> I am the Wolf
> I am the wolf
> who is the king of my home.
> I am the wolf
> who takes care of the land.
> I am the wolf
> who leaps all day.
> I am the wolf
> who rules all day.
> I am the wolf
> that drinks from the pond.
> I am the wolf
> who snuggles the kits.
> I am the wolf
> who loves to snuggle.
> Yes, I am the wolf
> who does all these things.
> Yes, I am the wolf
> who likes all these things.
> Yes, I am the wolf.
>
> *Madeleine*

Kevin decided that the best way to express his research about the king cobra was through poetry:

> Watch out!
> The King Cobra lies behind those doors.
> He will blind you with his deadly venom
> if you enter.
> His body will rear up and form a
> spine-chilling hood.
> So just BEWARE!

Sometimes our students would pick up on a format idea. Simon read his poem written in the form of a letter to the class:

> Dear Grandmother Fog,
> Oh, how thick your white whipped cream is.
> Why do you cover the earth?
> Is the earth your child or grandchild?
> I can hear you whispering.
> Are you lonely when you can't cover the earth?
> Are you a ghost of the Earth's Grandmother?
> You look thick but still I cannot touch you.
> Please give me a response next January.
> From,
>
> *Simon*

We got many poems that followed the letter format. Connie wrote a letter to the snow:

> Dear Snow,
> I watch you every night.
> You are freezing ice.
> You are vanilla ice cream.
> Why do you fall?
> Is it because the clouds are frozen
> and they break apart?

When Galya came back to school after a week of vacation her gift to the class was her poem "Shells":

> Shells lying on the sand.
> At night they shine,

> The wind rustles through the sand
> To make waves.
> Shells lying on the sand.
> The sunlight makes rainbows on the shells;
> The ripples of water look like far-off diamonds
> Floating across the sea.
> Shells lying on the sand.

Galya mentioned that she came up with the image of diamonds after talking to her older brother, Vanya, on the beach. Every day for several weeks after that, some child would come in with a poem that he or she wanted to share with the class, too.

Poets in books are powerful mentors as well. Anna Claire, a first grader, sat down one Saturday night and in invented spelling wrote a poem at the computer:

> The foriste is groweing and groweing
> dasuling gren goweing up wol the tree segs its
> on sog. The culrfl weg of a brd flis up wol the
> brd segs its on sog. the wed hals and thats its on
> sog.

> The Forest is Growing and Growing
> Dazzling green growing up
> while the tree sings its own song.

> The colorful wing of a bird flies up
> while the bird sings its own song.

> The wind howls
> and that's its own song.

Anna Claire was able to explain where she had gotten her idea. A note her mother had included with the poem said, "Afterward, she said that she had gotten the idea from Whitman's 'I Hear America Singing' which you had read in class! My child-poet already influenced by Whitman!"

Our students' parents have become powerful mentors, too. There was Emily's dad, who arrived early on a morning he was scheduled to help at work centers. He was clutching several handwritten sheets of paper, obviously torn out of a notebook. Bruce wanted the class' help to decide which one of the poems he had written was better. First he read a rhyming poem about swings, and then a free-verse version of the same topic. The comments he heard were very honest. Zach liked the rhyming one because it was longer, saying "It painted more pictures in my mind." Evan disagreed. He liked the other poem better for exactly the same visual reason. Adam decided a poem about swings had to have a rhythm because when you swing it has a rhythm. It was clear the children took their job as critics seriously. Bruce must have found it helpful because he continued to share poems with us that he had written; showing us various drafts with crossouts, arrows, and additions. The kids appreciated knowing that even adult poets needed to try out various possibilities.

One day Lynn wanted us to help her with a poem she had written. She shared several drafts. The children realized she didn't start with a perfect poem. She wrote and rewrote, just like they did. She scribbled on her paper. She wrote in the margins. Once again our critics took their job seriously. They tried to help Lynn find just the right word. Simon suggested Lynn change "paw marks" to "paw prints." Adam said he liked a line from an earlier draft that was missing from a later version. He thought "Pooh Bear" worked better than "blanket." This started a discussion on the need to save all your drafts. Sometimes an old idea can be useful.

The children's comments were so helpful that Lynn returned with a sheaf of wildflower poems she had written. A small group of children gathered around her, entranced with the idea that they were helping an adult poet find the perfect word for a poem. They also recognized that this was an authentic experience, not some contrived simulation. Lynn, like Bruce, really needed our help. She reappeared several weeks later with the polished version of *A Child's Field Guide to the Flowers: Aster to Zinnia*. After hearing some of the poems about asters, bloodroots, and columbine the next step was inevitable. The children asked if they could illustrate her book. This, of course, meant lots of excited research into what exactly wildflowers look like. When Dane read,

> When Bloodroot sends up a white flag of truce,
> the long, bloomless winter agrees to vamoose.

he drew a tiny bloodroot blossom dwarfed by a forest of tree trunks (see Figure 3.2). When Erika illustrated,

> Because they are shy, the Violets grieve—
> see how they wear their hearts on their leaves?

not only did she include a pot filled with violets, but a border of alternating violets and leaves (see Figure 3.3). All the illustrations showed attention to detail and great care coming out of a sense of ownership of the poems.

▪ **FIGURE 3.2 Illustrating bloodroot**

▮ **FIGURE 3.3 Illustrating violets**

Because they are shy, the Violets grieve--
see how they wear their hearts on their leaves?

Some people were poetry mentors without realizing it. Chris Breuer thought of himself as a potter, not a poet. He came into our classroom one morning carrying a potter's wheel and some clay. He found a shady spot on our back playground, set his wheel on a stand and gathered the children around him. As Chris' hands massaged the clay, as the clay slowly changed its shape, the circle of children stood mesmerized and quiet. Into the silence, Chris brought his voice:

> The most important work I do with pots is inside my mind.
> The clay is part of me; it speaks to me.
> I hold a dialogue with the clay.
> I have to be still; the clay is moving.
> I have to respect the material.
> I have to be open to change.
> Something in me changes. The questions I'm asking change. The
>   materials change. And then the style changes.
> Every time you try something, you express yourself as an artist.
> You have to know when to stop.

As Chris' hands transformed the red clay into a jar, Chris, the potter, became Chris, the poet. Along with the visual image of the clay going round and round on the potter's wheel as the pot got taller and taller, our children could hear Chris' voice talking to them through poetry. Chris' pottery demonstration was also a good example of how poetry can be an integral part of whatever you do. Chris was thinking about making pots, not poetry. Yet, he created both.

The poetry immersion residency allowed our children to see themselves in a new light. Robby didn't view himself as a writer. For months he had written as little as he could get away with. The physical act of writing was difficult for him. He could never seem to hold his pencil comfortably. The letters never looked the way he thought they should look. Writing always took a long time. After hearing Lynn Powell read Bert Kitchen's *Somewhere Today*, everything changed for Robby. He started spending hours adding more and more lines to his own *Somewhere Today* poem. He discovered the computer could be a tool that would help him write with more ease. He dragged visitors to our room over to the computer to see his poem because he was so proud of it. It was also the poem he chose to include in our Poetry Anthology:

From *Somewhere Today*

Somewhere today a flower is rising like the sun.
Somewhere today a desert is hungry and thirsty.
Somewhere today an eagle is swooping down for food.
Somewhere today a peacock is spreading its 100 eyes.

> Somewhere today the grass is waving at people.
> Somewhere today two boys are solving a mystery.
> Somewhere today a heart is beating.
> And somewhere today a person is writing.

The structure of the poem helped to free the poetry inside of him. Robby became so excited about poetry that after another writing workshop he asked, "Can we do it again?"

Not all experiences were as dramatic as Robby's but the poetry residency yielded unexpected insights about many of the children. Camaris told us quite a bit about herself in her haiku:

> The child was laughing,
> but the inside of his body
> was still crying.

We learned that Zack had a problem walking home from school when we read his poem:

> I wish I were a
> walking leaf because
> I could hide from the bullies
> that beat me up.

When the residency ended, the children recognized that "Lynn had stopped talking, but poems still rang in our ears."

If we wanted evidence that the poems still rang in their ears and that poetry filled their bones, we only had to look at the poetry that was being written at home. After taking a walk in the woods, Madeleine had to sit down and write a poem about an amazing bush she had seen:

The Firing Bush

> The bush, the firing bush
> that looked as if it was
> blazing with flame.
> The red fire was as shiny as bronze.
> The red was as red as blood,
> above the river's edge.

Only poetry could express her thoughts.

Anna Claire was spending time at night reading through her writing notebooks that she had kept from first grade. Using ideas from her notes, she then wrote poetry, titling her drafts, *jrafs*. She also included the reminder note, *etet*, or edit. Her "Sound of Silence" speaks volumes.

The sownd of slens

by Anna Claire

wen I crol into Bed on a col nut.
I her a sownd. it is a sownd that ers
cant her. it is the sownd of selens.
I cund nevur Duscriv that sownd.
that is from you amgunshn
it is a sownd that is from your sperit
it is a sownd that segs you to slpe in silens.
Etet!

The Sound of Silence

by Anna Claire

When I crawl into bed on a cold night,
I hear a sound.
It is a sound that my ears can't hear.
It is the sound of silence.
I could never describe that sound.
That is a sound for you.
It is a sound that is from your imagination.
It is a sound that is from your spirit.
It is a sound that sings you to sleep in silence.
(Edit!)

These children had discovered, with Ashley Bryan, "that poetry lives at the heart of the wonder and mystery of language" (in Copeland and Copeland 1994, 72).

Chapter 4

Art as a Visual Response

To draw you must close your eyes and sing.   —*Pablo Picasso*

Children come into the classroom drawing pictures, even those who do not yet know how to convey meaning through writing. In October, after a trip to the Allen Art Museum, Charde, a nervous six-year-old who wasn't yet sure of the letters in her name, was able to draw a picture of her favorite work of art, the nineteenth-century "Feraghan Rug." Her picture shows she noticed the many fringes on the edges of the rug, the different design patterns inside the rug, as well as the fact that several colors were used.

On a later trip to the museum, Pito, a first grader just on the threshhold of literacy, was entranced by four big balls of twine filling up the corner of the main lobby. Pito wrote:

GLLFALNGLLFALSENNOGLPAEFTELNBSSABNAVE

The log was very fat and heavy. They needed a lot of people to carry it.

His words needed a translation, but his picture could be interpreted easily as Jackie Winsor's "Four Corners." His logs did look fat and heavy, with unraveling balls of twine sitting on each corner (see Figure 4.1). These drawings helped to make these students' thinking visible in ways that their writing could not yet do.

We value our children's use of art as a way of showing understanding, and we encourage them to think visually. In his introduction to *The Enlightened Eye*, Elliot Eisner writes "If the visual arts teach us one lesson, it's that seeing is central to making" (1).

We want our students not just to "look" but to see like naturalists. We want to refine their observational skills and to help them learn to look for detail. As the poet John Moffitt says,

■ **FIGURE 4.1 Pito's visit to the art museum**

If you would know that thing,
You must look at it long:

. . . You must enter in
To the small silences between
The leaves, . . .

from "To Look at Any Thing," 1966

Dan Kirby and Carol Kuykendall in *Mind Matters* argue that drawing can help you find those "small silences between the leaves." They suggest that drawing "slows the act of seeing, allowing time for new insights to develop" (1991, 105). Using these ideas as a starting point, we sat on the front playground, gathering fall images to keep us warm in winter, just like Leo Lionni's *Frederick*.

Our children were very familiar with the front playground. They used it several times a day. They played out front before school started. They spent lunch recess on the playground. And after school, many children waited there for their families. They thought they knew it well but, as Maxine Greene says, we came face to face with "shocks of awareness" (1992, 1). Sitting quietly and sketching made all of us aware, in new ways, of just what the playground really looked like. Sharon noticed swirls on tree bark she had never noticed before. Kathy watched shadows dancing on brown speckled grass and leaves scurrying across the road. Andreas thought that "clouds look like paintings." Ian at first noticed the "dancing leaves." Then he felt the tinge of coldness in the air, becoming aware that winter was only a few weeks away. Ian's sketch shows the wind whipping the leaves as they dance in the air, clearly being pushed away by an oncoming winter (see Figure 4.2). Ian writes:

> Gold, yellow, red, orange leaves dancing down.
> Crunching leaves being stepped on.
> Pink and red flowers dying.
> Coldness
> Winter coming.

Our students were looking at a familiar world in a brand new way, visually thinking and using what they had learned while sketching.

These experiences helped us see that we needed to provide more time and opportunity for our students to draw. We also wanted to find a way for our students to be able to refer back to their sketches, to reflect, and possibly to write about what they had drawn. The idea of the sketchbook journal was born.

Sketchbook Journals

The sketchbook's expansive white pages are very inviting. The eight-by-eleven-inch journals have a spiral binding so they can lay flat. To make the book even more personal, each child designs his or her own cover. Since we were studying wildflowers, many children chose to press flowers for their covers. We had books shining with yellow and red flowers. Purple violets poked through Queen Anne's lace. Rose petals vied for space with goldenrod. Kids couldn't wait to draw and write inside the covers.

We gave our students some guidelines about using the sketchbooks and about sketching in general: They could sketch whenever they wanted or needed in the classroom. They could take the sketchbooks home if they wanted

■ **FIGURE 4.2** Ian's view of fall

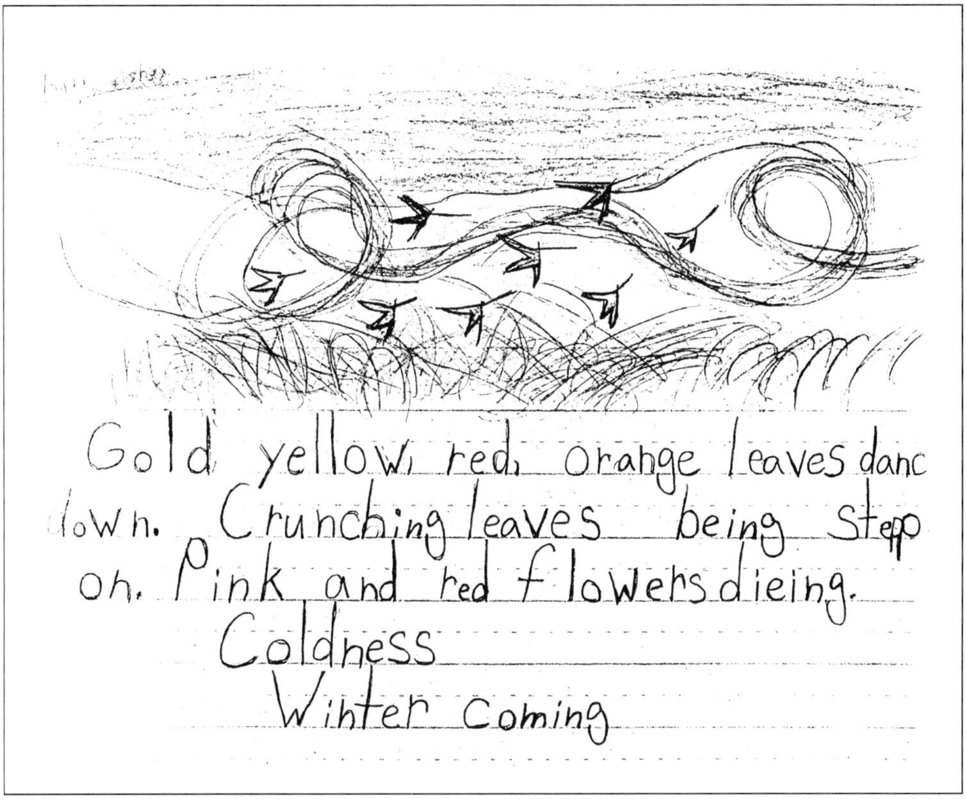

Gold yellow, red, orange leaves danc
down. Crunching leaves being step
oh. Pink and red flowers dieing.
Coldness
Winter coming

to share a picture with their families, or if there was something they wanted to draw. To get them started we built upon the ideas of Karen Ernst (1994) by introducing contour drawings. We suggested they draw without looking at their papers. We wanted them to pretend their pencils were actually touching the object they were drawing. As Karen Ernst says, "As I look at a person or object, I pretend that my pen is touching it, and I begin to follow the line of the subject letting my pen move along the edge, outlining the silhouette, going into the folds of the shirt, the wisps of the hair, the hands crossed on the table" (1). This keeps the students' eyes glued to the object they are sketching. Before they start sketching, we tell them to look once, twice, and then a third time at the object they are about to draw. As Kirby and Kuykendall say, "Looking and looking again is a way of life in the artist's environment" (1991, 86). They point out that Georgia O'Keeffe painted the same door of her Abiquiu home over and over again. She could not capture all the details in one drawing. Similarly, Monet painted series of pictures. In *Monet: The Artist Speaks* he comments on his approach to painting the sea. He says, "you have to see it every day, at every hour and in the same place, to come to know the life in this location." (Morgan 1996, 49).

Our children had to become Romare Bearden's "whale, swimming with (his) mouth wide open, absorbing everything" (from ntozake shange's *i live in music*), using all their senses. Then they had to write down their thoughts and observations, thinking in particular about what struck them or what made them wonder.

A trip to the art museum in April provided many opportunities for the children to make sense of the art they had "swallowed." Kara thoughtfully drew the marble sculpture *Lion Attacking a Bull* (Hellenistic, 3–2 century B.C.), being careful to use two different colors to help differentiate the two animals. She writes:

> **The Lion and the Bull**
> I have a question. What did the bull do to disturb the lion? Maybe
> because the bull wanted attention.

Kara articulated the idea of asking questions, saying. "I have a question." Not only did she have a question, but she also had a possible answer.

Ian was entranced by Eva Hesse's *Ladder* (see Figure 4.3). He spent at least an hour drawing as many details as he could, capturing the snaky shapes and the shakiness of the ladder. Pondering the sculpture, he writes, "I wonder how she got the cement to stay up?" He couldn't fathom why the cement didn't fall to the ground while it was still wet. How did it stay up long enough to dry?

Zach found Dan Flavin's *Untitled Neon Lights* intriguing. This sculpture is comprised of three neon tubes of differing sizes, one red, one pink, and one yellow. The question Zach asked is, "How is it art?" Many other children in the class were also intrigued by this particular sculpture and tried to answer Zach's question.

Simon's careful attention to detail in his drawing showed how important he thought this work was. He used a ruler to measure each tube and to make sure his lines were straight. As he worked he looked closely; the more he

■ **FIGURE 4.3 Ian's sketch of Hesse's** *Ladder*

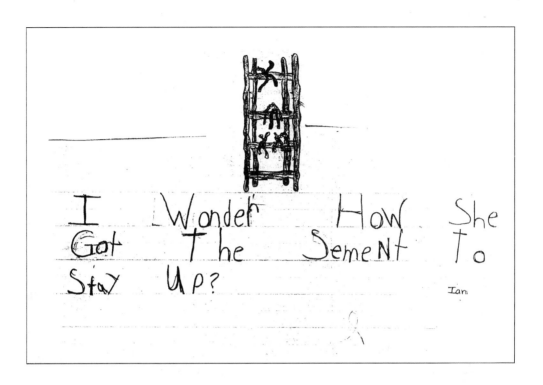

looked, the more he found. He liked the piece "because you act like part of
the painting because the color of the lights shine on you."

Reggie added another piece to the puzzle. He found the neon lights exciting
because "at night in the hallway, it is dark. [The neon lights] glow in the dark."

Leo's drawing had the last word. He drew a picture of himself in front of
the artwork, smiling broadly with his eyes as round as saucers. In a word balloon, he says, "I think that is cool!"

Together these children came up with ways of answering Zach's question
and of helping him view a piece of art that at first glance didn't even seem
like art.

By looking carefully, our children have slowed down the act of seeing. By
slowing down the act of seeing they have gained time to ponder and to begin
asking questions. As Kirby and Kuykendall remind us, "For every observation a naturalist makes, a question waits to be answered" (1991, 118).

As our children sketch, their books are literally littered with questions. They write down every question that pops into their minds, so some questions may seem inconsequential at first. Looking at a water garden, for example, some of the questions were: "Why does one of the roots look like a face?" and "Why does one of the roots look like a frog's leg?" (Alice) With practice the questions become more thoughtful. "Why isn't there any algae?" and "Why are some roots different colors than others?" (Simon). But it takes a lot more experience with reflection and questioning before the more important questions become apparent.

Kathy Short, speaking at an NCTE conference in Pittsburgh in 1993, talked about inquiry coming from questions significant to the learner. She believes that it often takes a while to get to the questions that matter. In the classroom, time constraints often mean a teacher stops just at the point where kids are ready to ask the questions that really matter. By giving our children time to sketch and wonder in their sketchbooks we are giving them time to ask the big questions, the questions that may not have answers, the questions that really get them thinking.

Not only do the sketchbooks give children the chance to reflect while they are drawing, but the sketchbook format also allows children to reflect months later. Looking back through their sketchbooks, they might notice something they hadn't noticed before. Karen Ernst says, "I use the drawing to help me notice first, then look closer, to move inside where my experience is" (1994, 1). We were reminded of this idea as we stood in front of Ad Reinhardt's painting, *Abstract Painting, 1962,* in the Chicago Museum of Contemporary Art. Reinhardt tried to eliminate color and brush strokes from his work until his paintings simply looked like large black canvases. At first glance, just like Flavin's neon lights, it is easy to dismiss this work of art. But by looking at the painting as Reinhardt suggested, by "concentrating on and becoming sensitive to its color and form" (from the painting's notes at the Museum of Contemporary Art in Chicago), blocks of color began to emerge. The longer we stood in front of *Abstract Painting, 1962* the more we could see in it. In the same way, the more time our students spent looking through their sketchbooks the more discoveries they make.

It wasn't only our students who made discoveries as they looked through their sketchbooks. We also made discoveries about our students' growth as we saw work in the sketchbooks change over time. Abby's first page of her book shows a small plant in an expanse of green peeking out of one corner. It is difficult to tell what plant she is sketching, and she hasn't included any writing to give us a clue (see Figure 4.4, page 78).

Her picture looks similar to the pictures drawn by other first graders in our room. By December, Abby's page looks very different: Her drawing has expanded to include the whole page. We can clearly see that she has sketched the amaryllis plant. She's even included a small new shoot growing next to the main stem. We didn't need to read her title, "Amaryllis," or her mathematical notation of 22 cm to know what she was looking at. Also evident in her sketch is the book that was open next to the plant (see Figure 4.5, page 79).

By second grade, Abby's caterpillar diary sketch and words show self-reflection and advanced thinking (see Figure 4.6, page 80).

Michael, a first grader, tentatively drew a beech tree for his first sketch. His pencil marks are hesitant and very light. His picture could be a tree. It could be a plant. No leaves are discernible, just an outline of a bushy top. Michael has, however, included the name of the tree he has sketched to help us (see Figure 4.7, page 81).

The difference in his drawings by December is remarkable: His lines are strong and provide contrast. Some are dark while others provide shading. He includes many details to help us envision the amaryllis he is drawing. We don't need his title to know we are looking at an amaryllis plant (see Figure 4.8, page 82). By the time he draws Clyde, the cat, in February of second grade, we're no longer surprised at the image he has captured with his pencil and crayons (see Figure 4.9, page 83).

Many children started to include detailed pictures in their reading response logs and other written work. Marvin's cartoon, "Running Marvin," told the story of a day without electric lights through word balloons and pictures. Showing only his eyes in the drawing made the point visually that there were no lights (Figure 4.10, page 84).

Maria and Mary Kate were not only illustrating poems they had written themselves, but were also illustrating the poems of other poets. After reading snow poems in *Sing a Song of Popcorn* (Beatrice Schenk de Regniers, et al.), they adorned our bulletin boards with snow scene after snow scene. Sketching as a way to share knowledge became apparent across the curriculum.

When we were researching animals, for example, several children chose to share their knowledge through drawings. Looking at Marvin's bald eagles, it is apparent how much research went into his sketch. One is struck by the eagles' talons grasping in midair (see Figure 4.11, page 85).

■ **FIGURE 4.4 Abby's first sketch, September, first grade**

■ **FIGURE 4.5 Abby's amaryllis sketch**

■ **FIGURE 4.6** Abby's caterpillar diary sketch, October, second grade

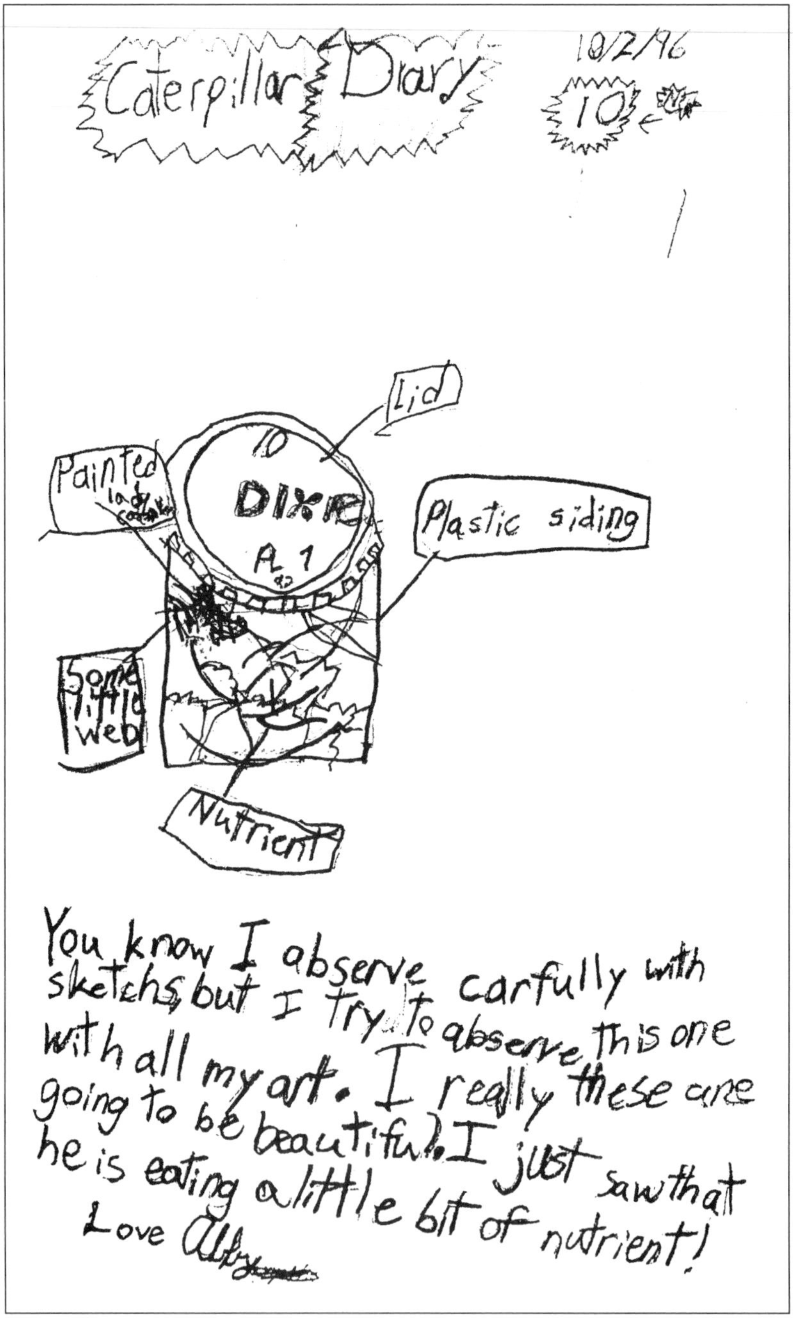

■ **FIGURE 4.7 Michael's first sketch, September, first grade**

■ **FIGURE 4.8** Michael's amaryllis sketch, December, first grade

■ **FIGURE 4.9 Michael's sketch of Clyde, February, second grade**

■ **FIGURE 4.10** "Running Marvin" cartoon

Natael's parrot perched on a branch clearly shows what makes a bird a bird, even without reading her words (see Figure 4.12, page 86). The arctic wolf who peers out of Daniel's drawing looks like he is capable of hiding in the snow and moving quickly if he needs to (see Figure 4.13, page 87).

Howard Gardner believes "when a culture begins to attend to children's precocious performances in a domain . . . one may discover unexpected gifts" (1993, 139). By making sketching an important part of our day we were discovering that many of our students had "unexpected gifts."

Sketching also helped us understand mathematics. Our students often used drawing to help them visualize a math problem. For example, when Natael was asked to explain what "pattern" meant, she used both words and pictures to get her point across. Not many people would have used vibrantly colored peacock feathers to illustrate this concept, but it worked beautifully

■ **FIGURE 4.11 Bald eagle research**

Marvin's bald eagles

I found out that bald eagles are three
feet long from head to tail, and they
are the symbol of the United States.
Bald eagles are the biggest bird
to fiy. Bald eagles are my
favorite   bird in the world.

to explain Natael's idea that "something happens over and over again" (see Figure 4.14, page 88).

Marvin, for whom math was a challenge, easily explored the concept of measurement by taking advantage of his artistic skills. His job was to figure out how tall the book table was. He was completely focused as he took out the linker cubes and snapped them together until they reached the top of the table. His accurate drawing of what he discovered shows that the table was thirty-eight cubes high, but his gifted artist's eye couldn't help also showing the plants and books on the table in minute detail (see Figure 4.15, page 89). The inclusion of art as a response had turned math into a welcomed challenge.

■ **FIGURE 4.12 What makes a bird a bird?**

by Natael

What makes a bird a bird? It has to
have feathers. It has to have a beak.
It has to have two legs. It has to
have claws. It has to lay eggs.

Some of our children used sketching as a way to help other children understand new situations. Kara, a second-year student in our room, was trying to make her brother, Aaron, a new first grader, feel more comfortable at the start of school. She used the tools of writing and drawing to accomplish her goal. As Donald Murray says, "The relationship of seeing and telling, drawing and writing is intimate, essential" (in Ernst 1994, vii). On manila

■ FIGURE 4.13 Arctic wolf research

paper she sketched two tables filled with children hard at work (see Figure 4.16, page 90). One table is labeled the discovery center. The other table is for writing. Everyone in the picture is wearing a smile, including Aaron. Kara is sitting at a table with her brother, as well as a teacher, who is commenting, "Good job, Aaron and Kara." On the back of her drawing Kara included a checklist for herself. She gave herself two jobs: First, talk Aaron into liking the teacher. (Was she concerned this was going to be an issue?) Second, talk Aaron into doing his work. Kara's sketch helped us see our classroom through her eyes. It certainly gave Aaron a window into first grade.

■ FIGURE 4.14 Natael's mathematical patterns

Mentors

As with poetry, music, and dance, providing tools, opportunity, and time to sketch is vital, but only part of what is needed. Providing experts as guides is also necessary. We discovered we had several mentors with us all the time. Some of them were students.

Marvin became a master teacher when it came to sketching. He was a much sought-after illustrator in collaborative efforts such as books or class newspaper articles. We would often find peers hanging over his shoulder as he showed them how to draw people and animals with delightfully animated faces, or bicycle riders that are a study in motion. Sometimes his lessons combined artistic skill with specific knowledge he had gained, as when he spent several work periods teaching other children in his research group how to draw birds perching on a branch so that it would be obvious that their talons had been designed for grasping.

■ **FIGURE 4.15 Sketching to measure**

Other mentors were as close as our classroom bookshelf. Beatrix Potter's books, *The Tale of Peter Rabbit, The Tale of Squirrel Nutkin,* and *The Story of a Fierce Bad Rabbit* had long been favorites of ours. We emulate her interest in nature and her joy in sketching animals as she studied them. She drew studies of animals as they "ate, slept, and played" (in Collins 1989, 23). One year we sketched animals that our classmates brought into the room for us to

■ **FIGURE 4.16 Kara's view of our classroom**

view. Michael's hamster, Speedy, burrowed into a corner of his cage, barely peeking out as the children watched. Andreas' sketch accurately captured him cowering in his cage, hardly to be seen amid the wheels and tubes (see Figure 4.17).

Kara shared Snowflake, an albino rabbit with red eyes. She had been writing poetry about Snowflake all year, and we were anxious to finally meet her pet. Kara's drawing shows Snowflake on alert, standing tall, whiskers quivering. A few weeks after Snowflake's visit to our classroom, she died unexpectedly. The children's sketches of Snowflake then became even more important to Kara as a memory of her pet.

Another mentor we found on our bookshelf was John Muir (1838–1914). Like Beatrix Potter, he was not only a naturalist but a writer, too. With only a wildflower press and a few books, he walked thousands of miles through wild terrain to study nature. We emulate his use of sketchbook journals to record "visual memories" as well as to record thoughts on nature (in Criswell 1994, 132). "As long as I live," Muir wrote, "I'll hear waterfalls and birds and winds sing . . . I'll acquaint myself with the glaciers and wild gardens, and get as near the heart of the world as I can" (in Landau 1991, 79). Reading through his journals gives us ideas of how to approach our own sketchbooks. We also come face to face with someone who feels passionately about nature and then acts on that passion. In making a strong case for preserving natural wilderness areas, John Muir helps us gain a respect for the environment. At the same time that he is acting as our artistic instructor, Muir is also educating us in the care of the natural world.

Artist and naturalist Jim Arnosky is a sketching mentor, too, teaching us through books and sometimes through videos. "Drawing from nature," he says, "is discovering the upside down scene through a water drop" (1982). In books like *Drawing from Nature* and *Sketching Outdoors in Winter* he gives us advice about the best way to capture nature: "Train yourself to include in your sketches only those details you can actually see" (1988b, 8). Good advice for us since many of our children at the beginning of the year include the sun in every sketch they draw, whether we are inside or outside! He also includes technical advice: "I use the thin edge of my eraser to create light-colored trees" (1988b, 8); "When you draw a footprint, start by sketching the overall shape of the impression" (1988a, 10). His black-and-white sketches are not only examples we can follow in our own sketchbooks, but are proof that his advice works.

■ **FIGURE 4.17 Speedy the hamster**

These mentors help us see that sketching is an entryway to experiencing
and appreciating the world; they help make the sketchbook journals a larger
part of the children's lives. When Michael's family went to the dinosaur display at French Creek Reservation, he had to take his sketchbook and pencil
along. Not only did he sketch the dinosaurs, but he then used those sketches
at home to write a story. Michael's mom writes, "Then in the car and at home
he wanted to write a dinosaur story and he had his sketches to help him."
Michael did not see sketching as only a school activity. He used drawing as a
tool to help him make sense of the world wherever he was.

Breakthrough

One of the most exciting aspects of using art as a visual response is that the
results we are seeing seem to support our belief that integrating the arts more
fully helps to draw into the learning circle those students who are still in the
margins. Marvin, whose work can be found throughout this chapter, is a
good case study to illustrate this point.

Marvin entered the first year of our two-year program an excited, engaging, verbal child. He was extremely observant of the world around him and
related easily to peers and adults. He seemed to be equipped with all the tools
needed to become a successful student. But learning for Marvin turned out to
be an endless series of frustrations—for student and teachers. In spite of his
verbal ability Marvin could not connect with what we were saying when we
talked about the reading and writing process as ways of making meaning.
His early attempts at communication that you see in his story about his birthday are indicative of that frustration (see Figure 4.18). For a long time Marvin's reading and writing progress limped along.

It wasn't until visual art became such an integral part of our curriculum—providing the time for Marvin to develop his artistic gifts—that things
began to improve. Not only did he use his considerable drawing skills to
communicate his understanding about a concept, but he seemed to be finding it easier to communicate through reading and writing (see Figure 4.19).

It took a while to grasp the connection, but eventually we understood the
way art provided a breakthrough in his language learning. When Marvin
first listened to us talk about reading and writing as making meaning he had
no real frame of reference with which to deal with that information, so no significant connection was made. *His* primary way of making meaning was
visual. It wasn't until he saw that his way of representing understanding was

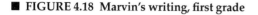

▮ **FIGURE 4.18 Marvin's writing, first grade**

valid that he could use this visual method of making meaning as a frame of reference in understanding the reading and writing process.

In an article in *Arts as Education* entitled "Working from the Inside Out," Margot Grallert comments that "by communicating a personal experience through artwork . . . students discover that their hands know a lot that their heads didn't know they knew" (1992, 88).

Making a valid place for his preferred style of learning so that his hands could tell us what his head knew not only helped Marvin make sense of his learning world, it also meant a significant growth in confidence and self-esteem. All of the talents we had noticed when he first entered the program

▪ **FIGURE 4.19** Marvin's writing, second grade

The Praying mantis Was big
And It was CliimBing up the
glass it was Fun Looking
at the Praying mantis.

began to surface, and his quick mind and marvelous sense of humor began to show through in illustrated work alive with character and detail.

The effectiveness with which Marvin had learned to use his skill in visual art to help him develop his skills in the more traditional reading and writing areas became clear when we looked at the results of the research he did during our artist workshop immersion (see Chapter 5). By combining his considerable artistic talent with his growing confidence in his ability to communicate through the written word, Marvin produced an impressive research quilt that explained the life and style of Leonardo da Vinci. Listening to him speak with pride to parents who attended our Open Room Art Museum Opening, confidently sharing his knowledge about the artist, it was clear that Marvin had discovered a bridge to learning.

That experience for Marvin came about because he and the other students in our classroom had spent several weeks immersed in a world where all of their learning was framed with the visual arts. These concentrated periods of time we call immersion workshops are an exciting direction our teaching has taken, and they are what we turn to now in Part 2.

Part 2

Introduction to Art and Music Immersion Workshops

The sense of discovery and excitement that pervades a classroom is not simply a set of words; it is a set of qualities, including a sense of energy that must somehow be made palpable through prose.   —*Elliot Eisner,* The Enlightened Eye

Nothing conveys the sense of energy and excitement of which Eisner speaks better than the immersion workshops our students experience at the end of each of the two years they are with us. Immersion workshops were born of the belief that children must have sustained time to explore other perspectives, time to explore the ways creative minds think about the world, time to experience the worlds of artists, musicians, and dancers from within those specialized areas.

The idea of the artist workshop first began to take shape when we visited University School as part of a yearlong pen pal project. Elliot Eisner, speaking at NCTE in 1994, said that art allows us to redefine ourselves and to enter into a world of possibilities that didn't exist prior to working on that piece of art. The second graders in Ray Levi and Linda Zelazny's classes at University School were involved in research studies of artists that opened our eyes to Eisner's world of possibilities.

At the same time we were collaborating with Ray and Linda we were reading Maxine Greene, who believes, "We ought to reach out to establish ateliers, studios, places where music can be composed and rehearsed, where poems and stories can be read" (1992, 16). We began to picture an artist studio where children would have time to explore different perspectives, time to experience the world of the artist.

Howard Gardner, too, moved us further along in our thinking, as he imagined a new kind of classroom: "Imagine an environment in which youngsters at the age of seven or eight, in addition to—or perhaps instead of—attending a formal school, have the opportunity to enroll in a children's museum, a science museum, or some kind of discovery center or exploratorium. As part of this educational scene, adults are present to actually practice the disciplines or crafts represented by the various exhibitions" (1991, 200).

We couldn't enroll our students in a children's museum or a science museum, but we could create an art museum-like environment in the classroom. We could certainly invite community artists to take part in our immersion process.

The immersion idea dominated our thinking more and more, but the artist workshop was born out of a single experience that captured the imagination of our students. We had just watched the "Art Chest" show on PBS, which featured Van Gogh, and afterward, our students spent several work periods exploring his painting style. They were completely involved as we read about this artist and tried to feel what it was like to see the world through his eyes. As we reflected on our work Claire seemed to speak for everyone when she sighed, "I wish we could study lots more artists." With her request echoing in our heads, we formally opened the doors to our artist studio.

Rich experiences generate other rich experiences, and our journey toward an opera workshop grew directly out of the exciting experiences our students had with the immersion in artist workshop. We had witnessed the lasting benefits our students had derived from getting inside the skins of artists and looking at learning through their eyes. Such an experience at the end of the year had allowed them to integrate all of their skills and had opened up entirely new ways of approaching learning. We began to think about possibilities for a parallel immersion experience for the alternate year in our two-year program. As we began to integrate music and dance more fully into the curriculum, the idea began to form that a music immersion workshop with opera as a framework could provide that experience.

Our detailed descriptions of our two immersion workshops will help you see how we addressed our language arts curriculum by weaving reading, writing, and research skills into our artist and opera studies. We explain how we integrate math through a study of two- and three-dimensional shapes, patterns, and spatial relations and how we work on science concepts through a study of light, color, and sound. And throughout the telling we hope you will see how we weave the individual threads of music, movement, and the visual arts into this tapestry that we call immersion workshop.

Elliot Eisner (1991) makes a telling point about descriptions of practice in the classroom: "To understand what goes on in schools and classrooms requires sensitivity to how something is said and done, not only to what is said and done" (19).

With that thought in mind, we invite you now into our workshops.

Chapter 5

Artist Workshop

The guide at the Art Institute of Chicago stopped in front of the painting of the *Old Guitarist*. He was unaware of all the people that had begun to gather around him, so intent was he on discussing Picasso's blue period. His group proceeded to follow him from picture to picture through the museum. An ordinary scene at an art museum? No. The guide, in this case, was an eight-year-old boy. Matthew's comments to his parents about Picasso's paintings were so vivid that a group of Japanese tourists spent the day following him around the museum.

We fill our room with paintings, posters, and sculptures. Van Gogh's *The Starry Night* jostles Monet's *Water Lilies*. Picasso's *Three Musicians* nudges Georgia O'Keeffe's *Poppies*. Eventually, it's not the work of masters, but the children's *own* work that will take over the room. Art books spill out from the book shelves. Bjork and Anderson's *Linnea in Monet's Garden*, dePaola's *The Art Lesson* and Grooms' *Ruckus Rodeo* beg to be read. Often these books capture the imagination of children who have fervently refused to be captivated by literature. We purposely read books aloud that will get our students excited about arts and artists.

We invite children to try painting in the styles of different artists. As Karen Ernst says, "Just as literature provided models in the writers workshop, the work of artists in the artists workshop provided students with models for technique and style" (1994, 82). We are following in the footsteps of many well-known artists by trying on the styles of other masters.

When Edgar Degas, for example, was eighteen he received permission to make copies at the Louvre. His copy of Nicolas Possin's *The Rape of the Sabines* gave Degas an opportunity to practice leg and arm movements. Copying the great masters and trying on their techniques helped Degas learn to capture movement. In his paintings and sculptures dancers are seen in various poses: putting on a stocking or raising the sole of a foot. Degas was able to take Possin's ideas and build on them, just as we hope our children will be able to use their mentor's ideas as a scaffold on which to climb toward new levels of thinking about their learning.

Not only do we want children to try on the style of famous artists, but as Gardner suggests we also want them to spend time with community members, who "actually practice the disciplines or crafts" (1991, 200). This particular aspect of the workshop changes each time we do it, depending on the makeup of the community at that time. One year a parent shared her stained glass making techniques. We sat mesmerized as Nadia soldered pieces of lead-wrapped glass together. Another year we asked Dave Neamand, who was substituting as a custodian in the schools, if he would share his silver engraving expertise with us. The class watched, entranced as Dave transformed a sheet of silver into a necklace, expertly moving his gloved hands to make three different cuts, encouraging the silver to catch the light and reflect it.

Howard Gardner has noted that although children around six or seven years of age are not aware of differences in artistic style, they learn quickly: "A few weeks of training, however, in which children look at paintings and are directed to notice stylistic features produce a dramatic increase in their sensitivity to artistic styles" (1980, 214). By giving children the opportunity to walk around in the skins of many different artists, we are helping them to become more sensitive to differences in artistic styles and, consequently, to different ways of looking at the world.

The children discover what it is like to work and create as Mondrian, O'Keeffe, Van Gogh, Monet, and Matisse. We provide the media to help children try on the styles of these artists. Ivory Snow soap gives tempera paint the thick texture of a Van Gogh painting. Pastel chalks turn ordinary construction paper into a Monet water-lily pond. Magic markers and rulers transform our canvases into Mondrians. Cutting out repeating designs and gluing them carefully on paper create Matisse-like cutouts. Painting live poppies makes us feel as if Georgia O'Keeffe has been invited to our room.

We use the best quality materials we can find: Our watercolor paper is premium grade. Our brushes are sable-tipped. By using good materials children get the idea the work they are doing is valuable. Linda Rief, in talking about the art materials her children use, says she makes "sure the students had top-quality acrylics and the best brushes. We wanted the students to know their art was important right from the start" (1992, 151). Many stores in our community are happy to help provide these materials; often you just have to ask. We walked into a bookstore just at the right moment one year. A large order of sample paintbrushes had arrived, and the store wasn't sure what to do with them. We left the co-op not only with fifty free, high quality paintbrushes, but a videotape explaining how best to take care of them! Minigrants have also supplied needed funds when we've been unable to pay for supplies ourselves.

Several weeks into the workshop we usually begin to hear conversations about art going on all over the room. Eric and Adam read about Picasso and laugh as they make discoveries about his painting *Three Musicians.* We hear kids arguing, "It was the rose period next, not . . ." Those conversations continue at home, as the lines between home and school become blurry. Tonia's Mom came in to help and commented that the dinner conversation the night before had been all about Monet. After a Georgia O'Keeffe poppies project Emily's mother noted that "we saw poppies and Emily's first thought was to tell you about it." Children discovered Van Gogh paintings cropping up all over. In a letter to us, Anna's father observed:

> Anna spots a tall bush . . . which was at that moment being beautifully carved up by the early evening sun. "That's just like Van Gogh would paint it," she chirps up from the back seat.

Not only are the walls between school and home tumbling down, but the walls between school and community are dissolving as the Allen Memorial Art Museum becomes our second home. In a talk at the Cleveland Children's Museum in 1988, writer/educator Richard Lewis spoke about the importance of scheduling several visits to a museum, rather than just one. On a first visit children often are busy looking at the ceiling, at the heating pipes, at the floor—not at what teachers had planned for them to notice. After several visits the students are ready to start thinking about the artwork. Based on that advice, we start visiting the art museum in September, and return five or six times throughout the year. Six different museum trips, each with a different focus, help our children grow as artists.

Our students oohed and aahed as they walked into each new room of the museum on our first visit to see self-portraits. Araka's involuntary response, "This is cool," echoed the thinking of many of our children. When we returned each child wrote and drew about his or her impressions. Simon's account let us know that he was busy looking around, but not necessarily at what the docent was talking about. He chose to draw a picture that wasn't on our tour:

> I like this 3-D painting I saw in the art museum. When we were looking at a man I saw this painting.

The docent was showing us a painting of Ernst Ludwig Kirchner's *Self-Portrait as Soldier.* Simon, instead, noticed the three-dimensional painting.

Adam, too, was paying attention to other works of art, rather than the pieces the docent was sharing:

I saw a chest and it had beautiful wood carvings on it in the middle there was a head and on the side there were vines and leaves. Next time we go to the art museum I'm going to ask about it!

Adam had looked at the chest long enough to notice the detailed work of a head in the middle, and vines and leaves on the sides. His writing helped us recognize another advantage of many visits to the same museum: Adam was already planning what he was going to ask about on our next trip.

When we returned in October paintings the children hadn't noticed on our first trip suddenly became visible to them. The amount of art in any museum can be overwhelming. By visiting several times the children were able to digest more works of art. Frank Stella's work *Ram Gangra* was hanging high up on a wall. Several children asked if it had been there on our previous trip because they hadn't realized it was there.

By the time our artist workshop started, our children already knew their way around the Allen Memorial Art Museum. When we announced we were going to the art museum, a cheer went up in the room. On our previous visits we had focused on self-portraits, patterns, the family, and human relations. To start our workshop we wanted the children to think about *possibilities*. What type of art did they want to study? Sculpture? Landscapes? Still lifes? Modern art? What artist did they want to learn more about? What did they need to make a painting? This trip helped set the stage for our study of arts and artists.

When Robbie asked if the paintings we were looking at in the museum were real, we knew we needed to talk about the differences between what our children were seeing in books and what they were viewing in museums. Art reproductions in books have limitations: The texture of a Van Gogh painting, its thick gobs of paint, can't be seen in a flat two-dimensional picture. A sense of scale is hard to achieve. The massiveness of Monet's *Water Lilies* series, canvases too large to fit into an ordinary room, is hard to discern in a reproduction. Certainly the sense of being enveloped by the waterlilies is missing. The quality of reproductions varies, too: The color in a painting often differs depending on the book you are looking at. Reproductions in books can give children an idea of what a painting looks like, and they can serve as reminders of a work of art, but they can't substitute for the real thing.

Reading Integration

During our artist workshop, the entire day revolves around the visual arts. Our study permeates math, science, writing, and music, as well as reading.

Expanding the possibilities for making meaning into the world of the visual arts helps our students make important connections in their learning. Pito, while looking through a zoo book, noticed a picture of a bull with a lion. He jumped off the reading loft and announced loudly, "This picture reminds me of the art museum. It's just like the lion and the bull we saw. It doesn't have a mane, but it's a lion." Zach, as he walked in the room one morning, grabbed the *ABC Musical Instruments from the Metropolitan Museum of Art* (Mayers 1988) off the shelf, pulled Sharon aside and said, "I told my violin teacher about this and she said, 'I wonder what instrument they have for Q.'" Zach immediately turned to the Q page, and discovered the quena, a Peruvian flute. He couldn't wait to show his teacher. The children seemed to be engaged with reading for longer periods of time. Part of it was the delight they found in making discoveries. Tomie dePaola's *Bonjour, Mr. Satie*, a book filled with visual puns, was rarely out of children's hands. Our students recognized dePaola's illustrations as takeoffs on famous works of art. They realized the illustration of a cat strumming a guitar had to be Picasso's *Old Guitarist*. The Henri signature on paintings could only be Matisse. It is moments like these that validate our belief that "educational inquiry will be more complete and informative as we increase the range of ways we describe, interpret, and evaluate the educational world" (Eisner 1991, 8).

Mathematics Integration

As the workshop develops, we begin to think of our classroom mathematicians as artists. In the book *Read Any Good Math Lately?* David J. Whitin and Sandra Wilde cite Elliot Eisner's argument "that scientists and mathematicians are artists, like painters and sculptors, because they are involved in the process of form making" (1992, 14). It is a particular kind of form making, however, that includes an aesthetic quality. This aesthetic quality of math appears clearly in symmetry, geometry, balance, and patterns. Artists have always been aware of the relationship between math and art. Leonardo da Vinci "applied mathematics to all aspects of nature—even to the structure and movement of the human body—*always* with an eye to proportion. Expanding on the work of Roman architect and engineer Vitruvius (first century B.C.), Leonardo explored the suggestion that the human body could be constructed on the basis of a square and a circle" (Corsi 1995, 1).

Our study of arts and artists is a natural pairing with a study of geometry. We invite children to build shapes using Leonardo's ideas about geometry as a guide. Children explore the concept of shared sides and stable shapes as they use straws and string to build three-dimensional shapes such as tetrahedrons and rectangular pyramids. Leonardo's notebooks include drawings of geometric solids. Abbey, Eric, and Ian spent hours trying to make a rectangular prism that would stand on its own. The string kept slipping out of the straws. The prism would appear to stand, then droop ever so slightly, sag uncontrollably, and fall to one side. We watched their repeated attempts at problem solving, admiring their willingness to stay with the task and try new solutions. Everyone has a frustration point, however, and when we felt their thinking could benefit from a little help, we asked them to look at some pictures of bridges with us. It didn't take long for them to realize that triangles provide the stability in bridge construction. They quickly went back to work to apply their new knowledge. Loud whoops of joy told us they had succeeded in getting the geometric solid to stand on its own. These children were artists, according to Eisner, because they had created aesthetic forms using math as their mode of expression (Whitin and Wilde 1992, 14).

Not only does math come into play during math time, but also while the children are studying artists. Knowledge of how to draw accurate, two dimensional shapes is necessary for creating a successful Mondrian painting. Trying on the style of Alexander Calder means discovering the shapes that make up mobiles, as well as learning to find the optimal balance point. When Calder visited Piet Mondrian's studio he was entranced with Mondrian's red, yellow, and blue rectangles, saying, "he suggested that 'perhaps it would be fun to make these rectangles oscillate,'" or in other words to create mobiles (Lipman 1981, 47).

In *our* learning to make rectangles oscillate, the balancing act is always the trickiest for us. It was also difficult for Calder. In his writings he discussed some strategies for finding the right balance point. One possibility is to "put a disc here and then you put another disc at the other end and then you balance them on your finger," or to "begin with the smallest and work up. Once I know the balance point for this first pair of discs, I anchor it by a hook to another arm, where it acts as one end of another pair of scales, and so on up" (48). In trying on the style of Alexander Calder we follow his suggestions for creating mobiles that balance. Mathematics is clearly involved in this process of creating mobiles. Even more than math is necessary, however. For Calder, "A mobile is a piece of poetry that dances with the joy of life" (19).

Sometimes a study of artists results in a serendipitous math lesson. Rikkie, a hyperactive second grader, was mesmerized by Picasso's painting *Guernica*. After observing the picture, he wrote down his thoughts and reactions:

> Picasso was sad about the war and he painted a huge picture called
> Guernica. The painting is twelve feet high and twenty-five feet
> wide! It has weird people. The people look like paper.

After Rikkie wrote this in his journal he had more questions: How big is twelve feet? How wide is twenty-five feet? Rikkie had to find out. He took out the trundle wheel, invited a friend to help, and started measuring our hallway.

Math is also needed to prepare the *canvas* for art creations. A study of Faith Ringgold involved making our own story quilts. Our students used 18" x 24" oak tag to design their quilts. Eric had to measure accurately in order to figure out how wide his border needed to be. He needed to find room for the text above and below the central picture, so measurement was a necessary tool. Math learning such as this was ongoing throughout the artist workshop.

Science Integration

Science is also an integral part of artist workshop. As with reading, math, language, and social studies, we look at our courses of study to see how we can adapt them to the artist workshop. The science course of study is a natural. Many of our experiments, such as those that explore color and light, build on the concepts we are also exploring in art. Experiments with color, such as the chromatography experiment, allow children to see that what appears to be one color is actually made up of several pigments. By putting a dot of Magic Marker color on filter paper placed in a cup of water the children can see the colors separate out. Experiments with the spectrum glasses help students understand that white light is actually made up of bands of color. As children look through the special glasses they are surprised by the differences they see in incandescent light, fluorescent light, candlelight, and sunlight. The light box experiment helps children see how color and light interact. In this experiment children look through a hole cut in the side of a big cardboard box. We put several toys in the box and include a light source with color filters that can be interchanged. The children choose one object in the box to observe. They notice how the color of the object changes depending on the color of the filter. These science experiments—all done with inexpensive materials such as coffee filters we gather from home or the spectrum glasses we purchase from science supply catalogues—help children better understand the materials they are using to create their artwork.

In an experiment that allows the students to develop their aesthetic abilities and to enrich their scientific knowledge about the use of the sun's light to form photographic images, our classroom scientists collect several items from nature; perhaps a leaf, a seed, or a blade of grass. They place the items carefully on the special photographic paper and then hold the paper in the sun, without moving, for several minutes. You can tell when our children are making sun prints: All over the playground you can hear them counting to sixty, over and over again, as they wait for the sun prints to finish developing. In fact, Scott thought this was the hardest project we worked on during the artist workshop "because you had to count to high numbers like sixty and seventy and one hundred." The completed sun prints, in various shades of blue, not only help children understand how light affects the photographic process, but also stand on their own as pieces of artwork.

We can see the children using the scientific knowledge they have gained when they are working on art projects. Adam used what he had learned about color and light when he was designing an inspiration button. Before he used colored pencils to shade in his artistic inspiration creature, he took out a scrap piece of paper. He tried mixing colors together until he got the look he wanted. His rough draft not only included the outlines of his creature, it also showed his thinking about color.

By integrating science and the arts there are hidden benefits: Our children, who primarily see themselves as artists, begin to realize that knowledge of science can help them in their creation of artwork. They also recognize that their knowledge of art can help them understand science. By the same token, our scientists begin to realize that they can use their knowledge of science to create art. A bridge is being built from art to science and from science back to art. Once again, the learning circle is being enlarged.

Sketchbook Integration

Our scientists and naturalists continue the practice of sketching for understanding during the artist workshop. (Sketchbooks were discussed in detail in Chapter 4.) However, the study of artists adds a new dimension to our sketchbooks. Learning from Monet and other Impressionists, we want to "convey the play of light in the open air" (Bohm-Duchen and Cook 1991, 8). The talk during an outdoor sketching experience, as we observe a magnolia tree in full blossom, sounds just like an artist studio. In one corner of the yard Robby and Kevin are discussing where to stand to sketch the tree. Natael is looking at the blossoms, touching them to discover the secrets of the texture. Words like "rubbery," "silky," and "velvet" float on the air. Kara, walking to the tree, says, "I need the little details. I just need the little details." Simon, standing to sketch the tree, states, "I'm trying to capture the shape of the tree." Marvin, staring at the tree, notes, "This is hard to do. There are so many blossoms." Simon, holding a petal in his hands, says, "Now I know what colors to do."

All of the children were looking at the same magnolia tree, yet each sketch looks different. Brandon's drawing, encompassing the whole tree, gives the viewer the sense of just how full the tree was (see Figure 5.1, page 108). The magnolia tree can't contain all its blossoms. They are falling to the ground, drifting down from the top branches.

Natael took the opposite approach. Instead of trying to capture the entire tree in her sketch, she concentrated on one section. You can tell how closely she was observing because her blossoms are so detailed (see Figure 5.2, page 109). Each one unfolds in a different way.

Evan chose pencil to convey his impressions. Instead of focusing on the blossoms he noticed the branches. Each branch and twig gracefully twists and turns on his page. The texture of the bark comes through in his illustration (see Figure 5.3, page 110).

Upon our return to school, Emily discovered a painting of a cherry tree in Raboff's (1968, 1988) book about Paul Klee. She couldn't wait to show us the picture. She said it reminded her of the sketches we were drawing. Those sorts of connections helped the children realize they were doing the same kind of sketching that real artists do.

Because our students were enjoying sketching so much we planned one of our art museum trips as a sketching trip. The children had a clear idea of the pieces they wanted to sketch from our previous trips. Jamaur, Nate, Pito, Araka, and Anthony immediately headed for the portrait room. Many of these children have behavior problems, so it took them awhile to settle in one place. After some initial wriggling, they became involved in drawing. Pito was entranced with the frame around Michiel Sweerts' (1658–1661) *Self-Portrait*. He spent fifteen minutes sketching it.

Anthony, a hyperactive child, was also fascinated with Michiel Sweerts' *Self-Portrait*. During the magnolia tree sketching experience, Anthony had needed lots of redirection, encouragement, and advice. Even when he finished drawing, his completed picture looked undeveloped (see Figure 5.4, page 111). As Anthony sketched *Self-Portrait* he was frustrated at first, too, but as he tried to draw the nose he was able to work his way through it. Anthony became totally wrapped up in his drawing and sketched for an extended period of time. His finished drawing shows tremendous growth (see Figure 5.5, page 112).

❚ **FIGURE 5.1 Brandon's magnolia sketch**

∎ **FIGURE 5.2 Natael's magnolia sketch**

■ **FIGURE 5.3 Evan's magnolia sketch**

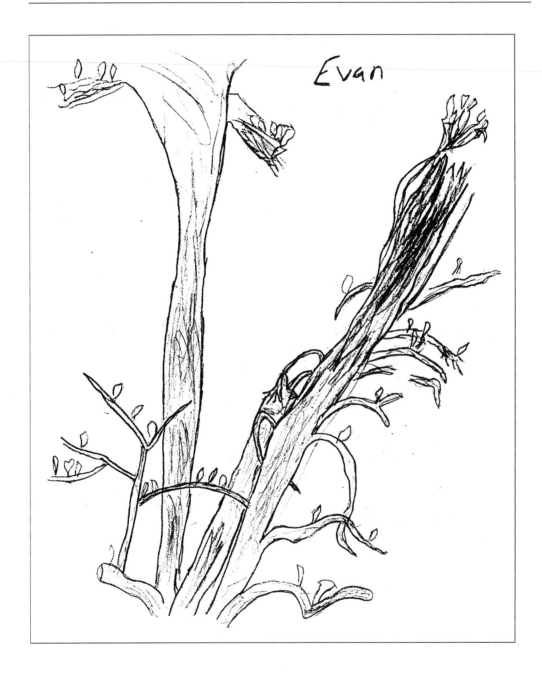

■ **FIGURE 5.4 Anthony's magnolia sketch**

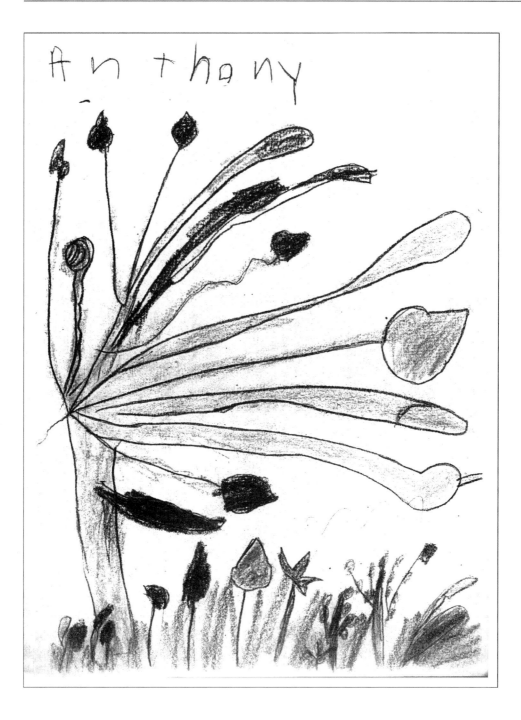

▮ **FIGURE 5.5** Anthony's sketch of Michiel Sweerts' *Self-Portrait*

Before we continue the discussion of the sketching trip to the art museum, an additional comment about the value of repeated visits seems to be pertinent. Children with behavior problems and museum visits are usually thought to be mutually exclusive situations because art museum guards traditionally take a dim view of less-than-decorous behavior. Repeated visits to the same museum make it possible for museum personnel to become familiar with the way students and teachers interact, and a sense of trust is estab-lished. Building such a relationship with museum personnel means that a teacher can work with them to plan experiences that will make these often difficult children feel welcomed.

A surprise for us was that the fewest number of our children chose to sketch in the modern art room. It had been a favorite spot in the museum on previous visits. Perhaps the pieces did not seem to be realistic enough for the naturalists in our room. However, the children who did choose to work there ended up with sketches that showed an artist's eye. Mary Kate's sketch of Frank Stella's *Ram Gangra* is filled with tiny details (see Figure 5.6, page 114). She noticed every curve and swirl of the piece.

The room that was the most popular was the sculpture court. The artwork that seemed to capture the imagination of many children was the large Chi-nese bell. Not only did Kevin's sketch include the Chinese characters that were inscribed on the bell, but also the sign that was hanging on the stand: "Installa-tion in progress . . . PLEASE DO NOT TOUCH" (see Figure 5.7, page 115).

Nika, a child who was adept at drawing, used her skills to show the same sculpture from two different perspectives. She was following in the footsteps of her artist mentor, Monet, by sketching the same scene over and over again (see Figure 5.8, page 116).

When it came time to leave the art museum, most of the children were ready to go back to school. Adam, Ian, and Leo, however, were busy sketch-ing the Chinese bell and didn't want to stop. Leo summed up their feelings perfectly when, gathering his materials, he said, "I wish I could stay here forever."

Writing Integration

Writing skills that have been developing all year are stretched even more dur-ing the artist immersion workshop. Reading response logs are filled with entries about the books being read. Natael, after reading a biography of Henri Matisse, notes, "Henri Matisse was not a healthy man. He had 103 birds!" On first reading it wasn't clear from Natael's writing if she was telling us two dif-ferent things she had learned about Matisse, or if she believed that taking care of that many birds could make you ill. Natael, however, is a child who thinks visually. Her picture of Matisse with wings extended and a voice balloon with the words Help me!!! leaves no doubt of what she was thinking (see Figure 5.9, page 117).

■ **FIGURE 5.6 Mary Kate's sketch of** *Ram Gangra*

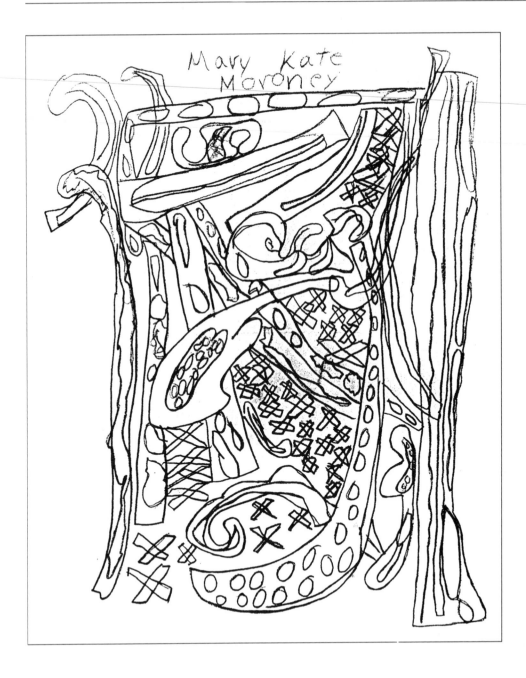

■ **FIGURE 5.7 Kevin's Chinese bell**

■ FIGURE 5.8 Nika sketching from two perspectives

■ FIGURE 5.9 Natael's thoughts about Henri Matisse

Art and writing work together to create meaning. Marvin analyzed Georgia O'Keeffe's style after reading her biography. He writes:

> She paints good. And she likes it.
> She paints a lot of flowers close up.
> Like it's popping up to you. She painted browns in the desert.
> And she painted from the inside out.

Marvin, who also thinks visually like Natael, tried to put Georgia O'Keeffe's images into words. This was a pretty difficult task since O'Keeffe herself said, "I found I could say things with color and shapes that I couldn't say in any other way—things I had no words for" (Turner 1991, 3). Georgia O'Keeffe's flowers, however, definitely look like they are "popping up to you." Marvin's insightful comments are an excellent example of the way he used his strength (visual art) to help him think about expressing his thoughts in words.

The artist workshop also allows for continued experiences with poetry. After reading Mary O'Neill's *Hailstones and Halibut Bones*, the room fills with color poems:

What Is Purple?

Purple is a soft plum, wrinkly raisin, smooth grape,
Good smelling iris,
Grape juice, grape jelly.
Dark purple makes me feel like a squished flower
that's just been stepped on.
Bright purple makes me feel like a newborn puppy
that's just seen its mom.

Simon

What Is Purple?

Violets sprouting in the warm spring.
Irises opening in the sun.
Quaker ladies with their buds bursting in the summer.
Quaker ladies spreading their beautiful petals for the morning.
Hyacinths closing their delicate petals for the night.

Adam

Perhaps what provides the most insight into our children's thinking are the "jump into the picture" stories. We collect lots of art postcards and set them out in a box. Children are asked to choose a postcard and imagine that they could jump right into the painting. What would they do? What would they see? How would they feel? Because of all the books we've been reading about characters entering paintings or paintings coming to life, our students are primed for this writing experience.

Domonique, a child whose demeanor was often hard to read, wrote about Renoir's portrait of the artist Alfred Sisley. Sisley appears pensive, resting his hand on his cheek.

> This man looks like he misses someone. They did not come back so
> he is sad, probably very sad. He is probably by himself and doesn't
> have anyone to talk to.

Emotion that is usually hidden comes out, first in the choice of painting to jump into and then in her writing.

Russell felt sad as he looked at Monet's *Fourteenth of July*. It made him think of his grandfather's funeral.

> My family is having a funeral and all my grandpa's friends were
> there. Me and my family were sad. My grandma was there. We
> cried. There was music.

Austin sensed the alienation and the feeling of loneliness in Edward Hopper's *Early Sunday Morning*. He feels cold and scared as he looks at the painting.

> In this picture, it is very early in the morning. I see that nobody is
> here. Maybe somebody took them or they are sleeping and it is
> quiet. The only thing that is noisy is the birds singing. I feel cold . . .
> and I was scared . . .

James, ever the pragmatist, was entranced with *Garden Landscape* by Ernest Lawson.

> Actually, I wouldn't *jump* into the picture—Then I would wreck the
> flowers. I would *walk* in so that nothing would be disturbed. I
> would walk around and see what I could see. I'd probably find a
> new friend—I think a lot of people would come there because of its
> attractive flowers.

At times the writing itself became the jumping off point. As Bryce wrote about Elie Nadelman's *Tango*, he became wrapped up in the musicality of his words: "If I would jump into the picture, I'd dance and dance. And eat. And hug. And drink. And dance and dance." His words just dance along with a rhythm all their own.

Sometimes art inspires writing and sometimes it is the other way around. The remember when . . . project starts out as written memoirs, and then develops into quilt squares illustrating one of the stories retold by the children. We start by asking the children to become researchers, collecting those stories their family members tell over and over again about things that happened in the past. The children interview parents and grandparents. Simon, a first grader, chose to write about an incident that happened to him when he was about a year old (see Figure 5.10). As his family tells the story, he was sitting in his stroller outside of a bakery in Oberlin, just enjoying the fresh air. A dog was tied to the bike rack, close by, waiting for his owner. Suddenly the dog became impatient and started barking loudly. The owner ran out of the bakery yelling, "Bad, Simon, Bad." Simon, of course, burst into tears. It turned out that the owner wasn't talking to him. He was talking to his dog, who just happened to be named Simon also!

Simon used his writing as a bridge to his art. In his illustration that he included with his writing the dog took center stage. Simon, the baby, is tiny compared to the enormous dog. In his quilt square version Simon and the dog are more equal in size. The dog's owner is in the center of the picture with his arms outstretched, not knowing whom to help. Simon, the dog, is barking, and Simon, the baby, is crying! Simon used his art to try out two different versions of this story (see Figure 5.11, page 122).

In-depth Study of an Artist

All of the ongoing work in the room revolving around the arts helps make children feel very comfortable with artists. Jeff, after reading about Monet, talks about his good friend Claude. Anna is on a first-name basis with Sandy Calder. Building on this sense of familiarity, we want the children to discover the special ways artists think and work. By studying one artist in depth, children gain insights into the whole learning process.

Some children want to study an artist they have heard about at school or in whose style they have tried working. Other children have an artist in mind that they discovered at home. Jacob had been to a Red Grooms exhibit at the Whitney Museum of Art in New York City. He had had a chance to sit next to Red Grooms' creations on *Subway* in the "one seat where a real human can sit." Red Grooms was his choice of artist to study. Tonia wanted to study Van

∎ **FIGURE 5.10 Simon's "remember when" story**

■ **FIGURE 5.11 Simon's quilt square**

Gogh after trying out his style of painting. Aidan chose to study Chagall because he was entranced with his painting *Paris Through the Window*. He liked "All the fantase"(fantasy) in Chagall's paintings. Adam, choosing Michelangelo, wrote, "I think it's amazing that someone can sit there and chisel away at solid rock and make it into a beautiful sculpture."

We had been concerned that we might not have the breadth of knowledge necessary to allow students unlimited choice in picking an artist to study. After all, even though we are passionate about art we are not art historians. Our students showed us that they were capable of constructing their own knowledge, as long as we helped to provide the appropriate resources. They became experts on their artists in a surprisingly short amount of time. During a discussion of Michelangelo the term *fresco* was used. Kathy said, "Oh, Zach, we'll want to find out exactly what the term *fresco* means." Zach, without a moment's hesitation, replied confidently, "Oh, I already know." He then proceeded to explain, "A fresco is wet plaster. The artist paints on the plaster." Neither one of us realized that Zach had learned that piece of information. Kevin, too, showed us that we had underestimated how much information our children had gathered. Several children were reading about the artist, Roy Lichtenstein. The question of benday dots came up. Before we could reply, Kevin spoke up. He said, "Let me show you exactly what a benday dot is." He then found an illustration in a book that exemplified benday dots.

We let our classroom experts take over. The wonderful thing for us was how much *we* were learning in the process.

A research project of this dimension is not overwhelming to our children because inquiry has been an integral part of the classroom since the first day of school. Oral interviews, surveys, and graphs help our children learn to develop questions, gather information and analyze findings. The artist study helps children synthesize all their learning. Research is also possible because our children form interest groups and work as collaborative teams. As a framework for our studies we adapted a middle-school team research strategy that Susan Robinson proposed at the 1989 Indiana University Summer Reading Conference and that Gail Wood and Barb Enos further expanded for use with third and fourth graders (see Figure 5.12, page 124).

To help the children formulate questions, we meet together as a whole class to create a web. We brainstorm ideas and try to think of everything we want to know about our artists. All of the reading about artists helped the children create this "Wonderings About Artists Web." As Donald Graves says in *Investigate Nonfiction*, "Most questions come from what we already know" (1989, 89).

Wonderings About Artists Web

When were the artists born?

When did the artists die?

Where were the artists born?

Where did the artists live when they were creating their art?

▮ FIGURE 5.12 Team research (Gail Wood and Barb Enos, adapted from Susan Robinson, 1989)

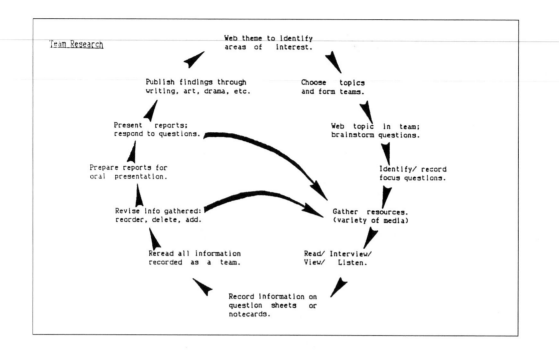

When did they decide to become artists?
What did they do before they were artists?
What were their periods called?
What materials do the artists use?
What are the artists' styles?
Do all artists change their styles?
Why do artists change their styles?

After generating these types of questions children interested in studying the same artist meet together as a team. The class web gives teams the support they need to come up with four or five questions about their own artists. Questions are written on index cards, with only one question per card. All members of the team end up with the same questions so that they can work on the research together.

Graves reminds us that there is a danger in formulating all the questions in advance, saying "the child will read only with a view to answering a few questions and not to gain a broad understanding of the subject" (1989, 94). To help deal with this our children know that extra note cards are available for interesting facts that do not fit the question format. Because the children have chosen the topics themselves their enthusiasm for the research propels them to find out what they need to know to understand their artist.

After the questions are written it is time to gather research materials. Teachers and children bring into the classroom as many books about the artists being studied and examples of their art that we can find. Many books are now being written on a primary level. The children are able to read the Ernest Raboff series *Art for Children* and the Mike Venezia series *Getting to Know the World's Greatest Artists* independently. Because motivation is so high we have some children attempting to read adult books about artists. Even when the words are difficult to decipher the pictures are still accessible. Joel, searching for information about Michelangelo, found a book written in Italian. It didn't matter that he couldn't read the words. He could still learn about Michelangelo by looking at the photographs of the *Slaves* or the pictures of the ceiling in the Sistine Chapel. Because the material was sometimes difficult and so exciting that the children couldn't wait to share their discoveries, many students chose to read with a partner. We read special books aloud to the whole class or to small groups.

Some of our research materials involve CD-ROM programs for the computer. There are several programs out now that are especially useful: Microsoft's Art Gallery highlights the National Gallery's collection. It provides information on artists and also allows children to manipulate images to better understand the artwork. Voyager's With Open Eyes works similarly, but focuses on paintings from the Art Institute of Chicago. Children can look up information on particular artists or see reproductions of art they've been studying. A child learning about Renoir, for example, could discover that his painting *Two Sisters on the Terrace* uses expressive brushstrokes to describe the landscape near Paris. What makes this program particularly helpful for first and second graders is the fact that you don't need to be able to read to use it. If you click on the open mouth you can hear an oral explanation of the works of art. For those of you who do not live near art museums these programs can be a real boon. Although they can't substitute for the real thing, they come pretty close.

Not only can information be found on CD-ROM programs, but the Internet is also a source of discovery about the arts. Web sites abound, and new ones seem to be cropping up every day. Steven Madoff writes, "How big is this virtual art boom? From July through November last year, 4,850 artists, museums, galleries, and other arts organizations around the globe opened visual arts sites in the Yahoo! directory" (1996). From our room in Oberlin, Ohio, we can travel to the Louvre in Paris (http://www.paris.org.:80/Musees/Louvre) or the Metropolitan Museum of Art in New York (http://www.metmuseum.org).

Another way of researching our artists involves going back to the art museum. For these research visits we tell the education director at the museum the names of the artists we are studying, and she arranges a customized tour. One year the director pulled two paintings out of storage for us. One was a Matisse, in a very different style from the cutouts we had studied, and the other was a Chagall. Our resident experts, students who had researched those particular artists, helped explain the paintings to the rest of the class. Of course, they also got a chance to ask the director questions about their own particular artist.

When we come back to school we are ready to start answering questions. The answers are written on note cards, one answer to a card, and always in the child's own words. Sarah, a first grader, in answering the question "How did Van Gogh feel about life?" wrote, "He felt bad. Because he ONLY. Sold a cople paintings."

During this stage of the research team members help one another answer questions. Group conferences are held and answers to questions read. Children share ideas about where answers can be found, and they also share answers with one another. Teacher conferences are held to offer help in locating more information, to discuss information, or to help read difficult material. At the end of this process everyone on the team ends up with answers to all the questions, as well as a record of the materials they used to find the answers.

When all the questions have been answered the information is ready to be put into draft form. Daniel Woolsey and Frederick Burton suggest teachers should not only be sharing books on the research topic, but also books that are good examples of possible formats for reporting their research (1986, 276). They believe that "informational books, especially ones with unique formats, may not only serve children's information-gathering purposes, but also lead them into the aesthetic realm of creative reporting techniques which can best be characterized as literary" (280).

Building on this idea we share books that convey information in a variety of ways. We read Ann Whitford Paul's *Eight Hands Round* and highlight her use of the alphabet as a format. We thought it might be too intimidating for first and second graders to think about using the whole alphabet as a framework for their own books, so we suggested trying an acrostic book just using the letters of the artists' names. We read Seymour Simon's *Animal Fact/Animal Fable* to introduce the true or false design. The format that many of our students are most excited about, though, is the story quilt. We read Faith Ringgold's *Tar Beach*, which had started off life as a quilt. Using this format the children can create their own quilts, complete with patterns and pictures. Their research can be written in a border around the quilt. Examples of the artist's paintings that our students think are reflective of that artist's work take center stage in the middle of the quilt.

Each child decides on his or her own final project. Team members can opt for different finished products. Even team members who have the same information written down on their cards end up with different finished products. Seymour Simon, when talking about writing science books at a symposium in Washington, D.C., suggested that if the five writers at the presentation "were forced to write a book on the same subject . . . five different books would emerge. Each author's voice is distinctive" (1991, 57). Each author's voice in our classroom is distinctive, too.

Writing one idea at a time on notecards is especially helpful for young students since it eliminates the tedium of rewriting and the confusion caused by trying to make sense of the arrows and crossouts that characterize most draft copies. The children simply lay out their research cards in sequence, shuffling or adding cards if the story doesn't make sense. In this way rough drafts of the final report are easily created. Although the warm weather is enticing and summer vacation beckons, our children work with an amazing intensity of purpose. One very satisfying benefit of the artist workshop has been that during the months of May and June, when many students traditionally find it difficult to keep their thoughts on school, our children can't wait to get back to their projects. We have even had parents tell us that their children were upset that it was the weekend. While not every child goes quite that far, the interest and excitement of this immersion experience keeps our students engrossed right up to the last day of school.

As they work to finish their books the children see themselves as teachers, explaining their subjects in a way that would help other children make connections. In discussing Red Grooms, Jacob (see Figure 5.13) notes:

> In one of his works of art there was a giant garbage can. It looked if
> it were getting bigger and bigger. There is strange perspective. I'll
> give you an example with a picture.
>
> That's perspective.

■ FIGURE 5.13 Jacob's explanation of perspective

In one of his works
of art there was a
giant garbage can.
It looked if it were
geting bigger and bigger.
Theres is st range
prespective.
I'll give you an example
with a picture.

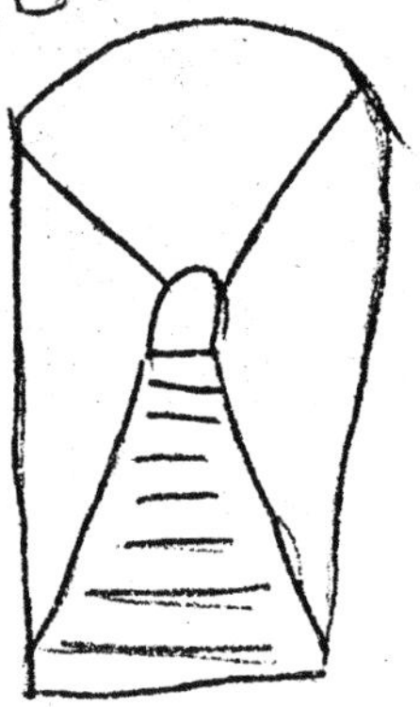

That's perspective.

Joel helps people understand what Michelangelo's stone fever is:

> Stone fever is when someone makes a work of art with stone and
> almost never stops.

Joel certainly had *Michelangelo fever* as he wrote his book.

Tom, an expert on Claes Oldenburg, wanted his audience to have a broader context for understanding his artist:

> He was born in 1929. And he's still alive now. He was born in the
> same year as Martin Luther King.

We had studied Martin Luther King, Jr., earlier in the year, and Tom was helping the class make connections between someone the class knew about and someone he wanted the class to learn about.

Evan chose to share his information in a true or false format with a twist. He called his book *Michelangelo: Truth or Hogwash?* (see Figure 5.14, page 130).

James asked the question "Fact or Fable?" in his *My Fact or Fable Book About Van Gogh* (see Figure 5.15, page 131).

> Fact or Fable?
>   Van Gogh was born in Spain, September 1, 1475. He lived to be 95.
>   Fable!
>   Van Gogh was born March 3, 1853 in Grootzundert, Holland. He
> lived to be 37.
>
> Fact or Fable?
>   Van Gogh, since he was rich, wasn't desperate for a job, decided
> to become an artist willy-nilly.
>   Fable!
>   Van Gogh *was* desperate for a job, and therefore, was forced into
> the position of an artist.

James was able to convey much of the information he had learned about Van Gogh through this format.

Kevin, on the other hand, thought that the best way to share his knowledge of Roy Lichtenstein was through a cartoon called *The Adventures of Roy Lichtenstein!* (see Figures 5.16 and 5.17, pages 132–133).

Paul wanted to convey his information about Van Gogh through a story quilt. In the center of his quilt he placed three of his favorite paintings. He

∎ **FIGURE 5.14 Evan's book cover**

■ **FIGURE 5.15 Fact or fable**

■ **FIGURE 5.16** *The Adventures of Roy Lichtenstein!*, page 1

∎ **FIGURE 5.17** *The Adventures of Roy Lichtenstein!,* page 2

chose *The Starry Night* in particular as the centerpiece because "the wind looks like it's swirling around in the night sky . . . it looks alive . . . the stars and moon look like they're really shining." Although a black-and-white photograph doesn't begin to do justice to his work, we wanted to include his story quilt as an example of thinking about research from a different perspective (see Figure 5.18).

Paul wrote his research information across the top and the bottom of the quilt. Then he added a border filled with an extremely complex pattern. The quilt required much planning, organization, and patience. Paul had to make sure his words would fit around his paintings. The pattern, which was aesthetically interesting, took a lot longer to complete than Paul originally thought it would, but he worked diligently day after day, completely involved in his project.

■ FIGURE 5.18 Paul's research story quilt

After our children have finished their research projects and we've tried on the styles of many artists, we visit the Cleveland Museum of Art. This larger museum provides access to many more works of art than the Allen Memorial Art Museum in which we've spent so much time. We arrange a combination of a docent-led tour that is tailored to the particular artists we've been studying and a self-guided tour. Because it is a field trip that arises from weeks and weeks of work and the children are so excited by the time we get to the museum there is no problem with behavior. They enjoy feeling like experts and quickly identify works of art.

As the docent led us through rooms to get to specific artworks some children started panicking. They felt like they were missing important pieces they had recognized. The children needed to be reassured that they would have time later to go back and look at the artwork they were interested in during their self-guided tours.

Seeing works of art by the artists they had been studying was satisfying. After returning from the museum Sarah wrote:

> My favorite painting is the *Water Lilies* I saw in the Cleveland Museum
> of Art because I am studying Monet and that painting was by Monet
> and I really like Monet and my Mom is studying Monet, too.

Some of the children were surprised by how different the paintings looked from what they had expected. Reggie was surprised by "the *Water Lilies* because I thought it was going to be little, but when I saw the *Water Lilies* it was big and it was long." Reggie had been fooled by the reproductions he had looked at in books. He made a good case for seeing real paintings as opposed to reproductions.

After all the museum trips are completed and the finished work is gathered we take time to think about and reflect on what we've learned. Simon was proud of his research book because, he said, "I was working so hard my pencil felt hot." Maria took pride in her quilt square because it gave her a headache, although, "A good headache," she said, adding, "I had a headache because so many thoughts and answers were swarming in my head at once." Mary Kate's sense of pride came from the idea of teamwork. She had "helped lots of people on their quilt squares." Pito didn't need to use words to tell us how proud he was of his *Did You Know Michelangelo Book*. We could see by looking at him just how amazed he was at what he had accomplished. Pito, a child with many reading and math difficulties as well as attention problems, had worked single-mindedly on this artist project. Once his book was completed, he spent every SQUIRT time on the loft, lost in rereading his manuscript. Every adult who walked into the room was treated to a personal reading.

Children felt a kinship with other artists as they experienced their own difficulties creating artworks. Designing mobiles in the style of Calder was hard for Maria "because it involves a lot of concentration and keeping the rod steady." Adam found the Monet water lilies difficult to create because he couldn't smear the pastels the way he wanted to. For many children the sheer length of time it took to finish the artwork was the most frustrating. Robby's lament was "I'm not done yet!"

We were also left with lots of questions, "questions crowded like a bed of stars," as George Ella Lyon says (1992, 15). Zach wanted to know why artists chose to be artists. Robby asked, "why did some paint and some make sculptures?" Kara's question was "How do artists decide what to paint?" Some queries were quite specific: "Why do they suck the tip of the brush to point the tip?" Nika wanted to know. Simon was curious about the places where artists were buried: "I would like to see if Van Gogh's grave had any flowers or what was carved into the stone or if they put any copies of the artist's paintings on the grave," he asked.

The last part of the workshop is a celebratory one. The children enjoy reading their books to one another but we want to celebrate our work with more than our classmates. In *Life in a Crowded Place*, Ralph Peterson writes of the importance of celebrating achievements: "When we celebrate in the learning community, we recognize that people have the power to incorporate the joys and achievements of other people into their lives. Celebration not only dignifies the lives of individuals and the group, it contributes to a sense of belonging" (39). These children understood what Ralph Peterson meant about the importance of celebration, so they decided to open the doors to our Open Room Museum of Art, complete with a tour book written by the artists themselves. The room was alive with color. Mondrian red, blue, and yellow paintings stood next to enormous Georgia O'Keeffe poppies. Drawings and paintings in Van Gogh's style nestled next to Monet's water lilies. Matisse cutouts adorned the walls. The Claes Oldenburg giant pencil had a place of honor in the back of the room. Alexander Calder mobiles hung from the ceiling. Original artist research books and quilt stories were prominently displayed. Geometric sculptures filled tables and the science area overflowed with color and light experiments. Even the computer got into the act. Our computer art slide show, complete with musical accompaniment, ran nonstop in the back of the room.

Children became the tour guides and showed their parents around the art museum. Many families found their way to our reading loft, where they read about all the artists the class had studied. At some point in the tour children and parents stopped at the refreshment table filled with cakes and cookies made from recipes found in *Monet's Table* (Joyes 1989). We all felt a real kinship knowing that we were serving the same refreshments Claude Monet ate during his afternoon teas.

The excitement was high when the research project ended. Evan wrote, "I like sports but I love having fun drawing. I especially like drawing because you can draw anything you want." Abbey wanted to find out even more about the artist she had studied: "I like Monet. I want to go to the Cleveland Art Museum because there is a Monet painting in there. It is a real big painting." Joel now saw himself as an artist. In writing about himself at the end of his book on Michelangelo he noted that:

> I began to be an artist in May 1989. I painted in the style of Van
> Gogh, Matisse, Mondrian, and Monet. I made a still life. I sculpted
> like Louise Nevelson. My favorite medium is wood.

Once again our learning expanded outside the walls of the classroom. Emily created her own art museum at home. She transformed the basement of her house into a museum filled with her artwork. Ariel used watercolors to paint flowers like the ones she saw in her backyard, as we had sketched the flowering trees at school. Not content to call her painting a generic *Flowers*, she searched through books and interviewed her neighbors until she discovered the name of the flowers in her yard. Ariel's *Patch of Scilla* synthesized much of what she had learned during our two-month theme.

Some families, recognizing their children's interest, planned vacations that included a search for art. Simon, who had written the definitive *Fact or Fiction?* book about Edward Hopper, went to New York to view the Edward Hopper exhibit at the Whitney Museum of Art. Anna, whose family was lucky enough to make a side trip to France before beginning a sabbatical in London, insisted on a day at Giverney so she could see Monet's gardens for herself. Matthew, who had studied Picasso in the classroom, went to the Art Institute in Chicago and became that impromptu guide you met at the beginning of this chapter.

Art, for these children, was not simply a subject studied in school. It was an integral part of their beings. They had learned to look at the world of learning through the eyes of artists.

Chapter 6

Opera Workshop

(Opera) is about something very basic—the human need to tell stories.   —*Charles Fowler*, MUSIC! WORDS! OPERA!

When we first decided to explore the possibilities of immersion in opera workshop six years ago there were more than a few raised eyebrows. After all, opera, so the feeling went, is more than a little esoteric. Why choose such a complex subject as a framework for children's learning? Why not stick to the basics?

Such criticisms might have given us pause had we not witnessed the positive responses of our students to previous encounters with the fine arts. We had observed these children as they sat in a theater mesmerized by dancers who could tell a story simply by the expressive way they moved their bodies. We had seen their eyes open wide when they entered the art museum and came face-to-face with Monet's lyrically beautiful water lilies, and heard them laugh with delight at Red Groom's wonderfully humorous sculpture *Token Booth*. It was clear that they viewed the arts not as something esoteric, but as a natural way of experiencing the world with all of their senses. Their encounters with the works of masters, far from making the arts seem inaccessible, are viewed as one more way of learning from experts. The reality is that when we talk about opera with young children we are talking to people who haven't yet developed the idea that opera is supposed to be a rarefied realm accessible only to the privileged few. To them it is just one more interesting way to tell a story. Unencumbered by preconceived opinions, they respond to the power of the music, the rhythm and beauty of the language, and the glorious images of costumes and sets. Charles Fowler, author and consultant for the classroom resource guide *MUSIC! WORDS! OPERA!*, speaks about the power of opera:

> [Opera] is about something very basic—the human need to tell stories. No matter how old we are, we all rely to some extent on our

ability to spin tales. It is one of the ways that we create our worlds each day. We fashion heroes. We find our villains. We make up the episodes that explain our agonies, our delights, our hungers, our discoveries, our beliefs. Where facts fail to provide answers, we let our imaginations fill in.

But just as important, certainly, is our capacity to enter into other people's stories. With the help of our imaginations, we can meet intriguing characters and experience incredible journeys that transport us to other worlds and other times. When the story is a good one, we find we care, we hope, we fear, we triumph. Because of it, we *feel* and learn about ourselves, other people, and the world we live in. (1990, ix)

The idea that opera encourages students to exercise their imaginations is one of the great gifts of this art form, one that not only allows them to enter into other lives and other worlds, but also expands, sharpens, and hones their thinking about this world. At the NCTE convention in 1994, Elliot Eisner spoke eloquently of the need to nurture imagination:

The central term of imagination is "image," and the ability to form images that give us aspirations that exceed our grasp is what is required in order to build the kind of society we would like to live in. It is a fundamental human capacity. In fact, the formulation of intentions themselves requires a capacity to imagine what might be but what is not yet.

Eisner's speech touched on one of the real challenges in helping people understand the importance of integrating the arts into the curriculum. We expend a good deal of energy helping parents, colleagues, and administrators who are genuinely concerned about acquisition of basic skills to understand that creating environments where imagination can flourish *is* developing basic skills. As Eisner points out, there is nothing more basic to education than being able to envision a goal, to "imagine what might be but what is not yet." The development of imagination is a powerful learning tool students will need in a world that is changing as rapidly as the one we face as we approach the year 2000. Those of us who teach primary grades have only to look back over the last ten years to know that the children we teach this year will be facing a very different world by the time they graduate from high school. We need to help them develop the wide-ranging skills that will allow them to adapt to change. Creating school curricula that encourage students to use all of their senses and allow them to access all of their capabilities is vital to that development.

The study of opera, with its integration of several art forms, is one powerful way to do that. It is a rich environment that encourages students to use all of their creative skills including reading, writing, logical thinking, art, music, and dance. It requires students to employ all of their senses as they interpret the worlds created by masters and learn to create dramatic worlds of their own. It is a natural framework, a logical extension of the language arts experience. Opera repertoire is replete with opportunities for teaching elements of plot, character, and setting, those elements of story structure that stand out because opera, by nature, is dramatic in its telling. That idea, in itself, has important educational implications, but the richness of opera provides so much more. Our students, like the students of many of you who are reading this book, are surrounded by the power and beauty of language every day in the classroom, much of it so lyrical that it resonates long after it is read. It is language that longs for other outlets of expression—and opera provides that outlet. Charles Fowler supports this belief when he says:

> Because it is a multiart form, opera invites students to explore several of the basic ways humans communicate—through words, music, dramatic expression, and visual arts. As a form of human expression, opera challenges students to reach beyond speaking and writing and to think more comprehensively about their own ability to express and to communicate. (1990, ix)

Music! Words! Opera!

Once the idea of an opera workshop took root, we began investigating sources that might provide materials to support our endeavor. We heard about a program created by OPERA America, a service organization for professional opera companies. In the late seventies OPERA America had asked professionals from the fields of education, cognitive psychology, literature, musicology, and the performing arts to come together and discuss ways to introduce the study of opera into classrooms. Supported by a grant from the National Endowment for the Humanities, the group designed *MUSIC! WORDS! OPERA!*, a curriculum meant to be woven into existing school curricula. The result of many years of planning, it is a curriculum with far-ranging possibilities for helping classroom teachers enrich the learning environment and expand opportunities for the teaching of language arts.

MUSIC! WORDS! OPERA! is essentially a two-part program: The first section, entitled "Listen and Discover," is a complete curriculum in which children study an established opera, learning about the elements of story through what the authors call story sharing. In the Level I curriculum, designed for kindergarten, first, and second grades, teachers and students may choose to study *Hansel and Gretel, The Magic Flute,* or *The Child and the Enchantments.*

The second section of *MUSIC! WORDS! OPERA!*, entitled "Create and Produce," provides students with the opportunity of entering directly into the world of opera by creating and performing their own original opera, either one they write or one based on a favorite book or poem. The curriculum in this section is designed so that students learn to choose a story, write a libretto, compose music, and stage a performance.

Both "Listen and Discover" and "Create and Produce" are accompanied by comprehensive lesson plan suggestions, audiotapes, student study books, and information about resource materials. They are designed for maximum flexibility so that they can be used equally effectively by a classroom teacher who is a complete novice to the world of music and opera, or adapted to supplement the needs of a teacher who has an extensive musical background. Suggested time lines are also flexible so that the curriculum can be adapted to fit into existing classroom curricula instead of being imposed on top of an already full teaching schedule. Because it often helps to have a specific picture we will describe our experience with *MUSIC! WORDS! OPERA!* in detail, illustrating the ways in which we used that curriculum as a framework for teaching the concepts of our various courses of study. Along with many teachers from neighboring schools who have been involved in the program, we have found that the possibilities for integrating various parts of the curriculum into work with *MUSIC! WORDS! OPERA!* actually made for much more efficient use of teaching time.

Although *MUSIC! WORDS! OPERA!* is designed as a complete curriculum, there are several opera companies in the country that have combined their talents with OPERA America to provide a music mentor program that supports the curriculum. In our case, we have had the good fortune of developing a stimulating and satisfying relationship with the people of Cleveland Opera through Cleveland Opera On Tour. The role of the mentor, like the *MUSIC! WORDS! OPERA!* curriculum, is a flexible one that can take many different directions. His or her main purpose is to provide the technical musical expertise the classroom teacher often lacks, helping that teacher grow in new directions.

Opera companies with whom interested schools and teachers might build a partnership are an excellent source for finding a music mentor, but they aren't the only place. If your school is located near a conservatory of music or a college with a strong music performance program you might consider developing a partnership with music majors who can act as mentors. Asking the school music teacher to act as a mentor for the opera experience is an excellent opportunity to integrate *specials* with classroom teaching, and provide the possibility of forming another collaborative team. Our music and art teachers have become integral parts of our opera immersion experience and both specialists have commented on how they feel so much more a part of what is going on in the classroom. All of us involved see it as an exciting new direction for our teaching.

The mentors mentioned thus far have been professionals, but even that doesn't have to be the case. A mentor could just as easily be someone from the community who has experience with music and performance, perhaps a member of a community theater or civic orchestra group. It isn't necessary for the mentor to have an operatic voice. More important is some technical background and a passion for music that he or she can communicate to the students. We are constantly amazed at the wealth of talent that lies within most communities and heartened by the willingness of many community members to share their expertise with children.

Evolution of Opera Workshop

Preparation for the opera immersion experience actually began long before we even thought about the "Listen and Discover" section of *MUSIC! WORDS! OPERA!* In truth, it began the first day of school when our students walked into the room to be greeted by the strains of a Bach concerto, and continued as children responded to the language, music, movement, and sketching experiences you have read about in earlier chapters in this book. Those were the individual threads we were helping the children develop, providing time and opportunity for them to discover ways their eyes, ears, bodies, and imaginations could respond to artistic invitations to view the world of learning.

In the first months of the year our work was a general exploration: a variety of music and movement so that students could hear and absorb a range of rhythms and mood; sketching experiences to sharpen the eye and develop the senses; poetry writing to heighten senses and encourage imaginative use of language. Weaving through all of these experiences was an emphasis on developing an awareness of how music, color, and language affect our moods and responses, an idea important in understanding the world in general, and crucial to understanding the world of opera.

Mini-Operas

As we moved into the later fall months experiences began to take on a more specific focus. Creating mini-operas using familiar fairy tales, nursery rhymes, and children's songs served as a bridge to the more detailed study of opera that would come later in the year during "Create and Produce." The idea of mini-operas was the creation of our colleagues Ray Levi and Gail Wood. It grew out of their work introducing reading through familiar children's songs, the idea being that a child who had repeated experiences following familiar words sung to familiar rhythms would eventually begin to recognize those words in other contexts as well.

Mini-operas are an imaginative way for children to work on comprehension skills such as retelling a story, while providing an opportunity to develop creative and collaborative skills. The key to the mini-opera is that students learn to tell a story completely through music. We work on mini-operas after our genre study of fairy tales and folk tales, so that the children have already had many opportunities to hear and read multiple versions of many different tales. That genre study usually takes place in November, so in early December we begin to think about mini-operas. A full explanation of the steps to creating a mini-opera can be found in Appendix B. A quick overview here should help you get the picture of how the process works.

Children decide which fairy tale or nursery rhyme they would like to turn into a mini-opera, with those interested in the same story forming collaborative groups. We ask them to list three choices in order of preference because we often end up with too many children for one story and not enough for another. It is a good opportunity to teach a little about compromise and negotiation. Although every student would rather have his first choice, each knows there will be many other opportunities to make choices throughout the year, so with help (and sometimes a lot of talk) they are willing to compromise.

Once a group has its story, say, *The Three Little Pigs*, they go to work thinking about the characters they will need to tell the story and the words each character will need to sing. Then the children fit their words to a familiar melody such as "Skip to My Lou."

> Skip, skip, skip to my Lou
> Skip, skip, skip to my Lou
> Skip, skip, skip to my Lou
> Skip to my Lou, my darling.

In the hands of our first and second graders this might become:

> I am the first little pig
> I am the first little pig
> I am the first little pig
> I am building a house of sticks.

There is no writing down of lines and no memorization involved. Words may change slightly from day to day but that works as long as they fit the sense of the story.

All of the work is done during writing workshop and other language arts periods in our day. Reading skills, such as sequencing ideas, learning to retell a story, and choosing the main ideas to carry a story, are all addressed as children develop a simple libretto for their mini-opera. The goals of the social studies curriculum are also being addressed as children develop the skills needed to work collaboratively in small groups. Because some of our students have social skills that are still at a basic level of development, this small group work can be a challenge for all involved. The adults spend as much time leading these children through cooperative learning skills as on the creation of the mini-opera, one reason why we want this first experience in story telling to be a familiar and simple one. That way the children can also concentrate on the equally important work of developing the social skills they need to grow.

As they work on their mini-operas children begin to develop poise and self-confidence. They learn to sing out and to allow their actions and facial expressions to show the drama or humor of the story. Sometimes self-discovery is dramatic and humorous. We will never forget Karl, a very shy, soft-spoken six-year-old, who always had to be gently encouraged to take part in discussions and to speak in a voice that could be heard. When it came time to choose characters for the mini-operas he decided he wanted to be the Big Bad Wolf. Much to our amazement, and to the delight of his friends in the audience, Karl sang in a voice so ferocious that he could barely speak the next day. It was clear from the grin on his face and pride reflected in his eyes that he felt it was well worth it!

The development of mini-operas is neither a long nor an involved process. The entire sequence of choosing a familiar fairy tale or nursery rhyme, retelling the story to fit the music of a familiar tune, and rehearsing the mini-operas takes about three to four weeks of language arts time. The mini-operas are short, some only a few minutes long. As the children work we concentrate on the process of telling a story through song. Each day we gather to look at a few of the mini-operas in process so that the audience can help groups move forward by using critiquing methods similar to the ones mentioned in earlier chapters. After viewing the work-in-progress we always begin our critique by mentioning three things the group did well. Those comments are then followed by three questions: Did the group tell their story? Could the group be heard? What can the group do to make their mini-opera better?

We are not looking for a polished performance as an end result, but we do want the children to know that their work has a real purpose, so we invite parents and relatives to an afternoon performance of the mini-operas. The performance is very much of the workshop variety—no fancy costumes or sets. Students often ad lib new words as they perform their operas, but as long as the dialogue fits the story and the melody no one seems to mind. Parents are always thrilled with the creativity of the children, and our students always gain some new insight about themselves. Sometimes it is the idea that they have overcome the fear of performance; sometimes it is the realization that they love to act and sing; and sometimes it is the pride of knowing that they have learned to cooperate with other people.

Listen and Discover

With the experience of the mini-operas serving as a bridge we began our work with *MUSIC! WORDS! OPERA!* when we returned from winter break in January. Our choice for the "Listen and Discover" section of the opera study was Mozart's *The Magic Flute*, an opera full of charm and whimsy, and certainly one that we felt was quite accessible to young children. To prepare the children for the experience of seeing the opera and to begin getting their ears *tuned in,* we filled the room with the music of Mozart. We played movements from symphonies such as the first movement of the *Jupiter,* violin concertos and pieces for violin and viola such as *Sinfonia Concertante,* and of course, the overture from *The Magic Flute.* The music played softly in the background during SQUIRT time in the mornings; it could often be heard underscoring our writing workshop; it helped children focus their observational skills as they sketched; and it provided wonderful opportunities for visualization.

To learn more about the composer we read several children's biographies about the life of Wolfgang Amadeus Mozart. You will find several of them cited in the Annotated Bibliography at the end of this book. We also read several different versions of *The Magic Flute,* so that the children would be familiar with the libretto before they began to watch the video of the opera performance. It is an important step because many excellent performances of opera are often in foreign languages (with subtitles), and even when performed in English the trained operatic voice sings in such high registers as to make it difficult to understand. Our approach to viewing opera with children is the same approach we would take as adults: We became very familiar with the libretto before viewing the opera so that the story would be easier to follow. A particularly good version of *The Magic Flute* is *The Magic of Mozart: Mozart, The Magic Flute, and The Salzburg Marionettes* by Ellen Switzer.

To ensure that the opera study would flow naturally from the rest of the curriculum, we intentionally set the study of *The Magic Flute* immediately after our reading workshop focus on the genre of fairy tales and the experience with mini-operas that took place in November and December. This way the children have already developed a sense of the format of a fairy tale and they have certain expectations and can make predictions about what will happen in the opera stories. This preparatory background greatly enhances their experience.

The idea that work with opera grows directly out of work you are doing in the classroom cannot be emphasized enough. In Oberlin, for example, the third-grade social studies curriculum involves a focused study on the history of Oberlin that encompasses several weeks. Our colleagues Barb Enos and Gail Wood, who teach in a third- and fourth-grade team, combined the study of the history of Oberlin with their opera experience by adapting the folk tale *The Crane Wife* into a folk opera they called *Our Dear Daughter*. Using the information about the early years in the history of Oberlin they had gleaned from social studies lessons, the third- and fourth-grade students wrote an original libretto. Then working with a mentor from Cleveland Opera and with a student from Oberlin College who was interested in choreography, they added music and dance to their opera. The resulting opera was an excellent example of performance assessment in which students used art, writing, music, and dance to display their creativity and original thinking as well as their understanding of the social studies curriculum.

The pivotal idea is to mine the riches and unique qualities that often lie hidden within most communities, and then to study your curriculum to see how it can be adapted. If you live near a river, for example, there are possibilities for researching that river, connecting it with a study of the environment, and creating either an original opera or an adaptation of a story such as Jane Yolen's *Letting Swift River Go,* or, for older students, Lynne Cherry's *A River Ran Wild.*

The Appalachian region, where storytellers abound and where music has such a unique quality, seems rich with opportunity. Turning one of those stories into an opera could be a fascinating lesson in history and culture. There is also the possibility of adapting one of the beautiful books written with an Appalachian theme. One that comes to mind is Libba Moore Gray's *My Mama Had a Dancing Heart*, a book that celebrates family relationships and the unique beauty of the seasons in the Appalachian hills.

Big cities, with their kaleidoscope of sights, sounds, and rhythms provide a treasure for the creation of an original opera. You just need to stand back and look at your surroundings from a different perspective. The idea in creating student operas is not to groom the next Pavarotti; it is to help students reach inside themselves and respond to the world around them with all of their senses.

Because opera provides such an effective framework for teaching we spent a great deal of the "Listen and Discover" time working on language arts skills. One such skill is that of learning to retell a story. After reading a version of *The Magic Flute* we often sat in a circle and retold the story. A favorite way of doing this involved the use of a ball of yarn as a prop. Everyone sat in a circle, with one person holding the ball of yarn. That person began retelling the story. After a sentence or two she rolled the ball of yarn to another child who held the ball as she continued the story. She then rolled the ball to someone else and the process continued until the story had been completely retold. It is a deceptively simple lesson because there are so many skills being addressed simultaneously: The children must know the story; they must listen to each other because they never know where the ball of yarn will roll next; and they must communicate their ideas clearly. It also provides the opportunity for the aural learner to shine. Carrie, a student who was struggling to make sense of words on a page, displayed a real talent for remembering both the main ideas and fine details that kept our story retelling moving forward, and it did wonders for her self-esteem. When the retelling is complete, the intricate web of yarn in the middle of the circle is a graphic record of community participation.

Art Specialist

Retelling the story was one way we helped children internalize the story of *The Magic Flute;* using the medium of art was another way for them to think about the experience. As we read versions of the story and played audiotape excerpts of music from the opera, we intentionally refrained from showing the children pictures of the characters or scenery in the books. We wanted them to form their own images by combining the words in the story with the *feel* of the music. As they listened to the whimsical, light music that always accompanied Papageno's presence, they began to imagine what this birdman might look like. As they felt the majestic, commanding music that announced Sarastro's entrance seep into their bones they immediately visualized a person of power. And as they listened to the magnificent, soaring music of the Queen of the Night they envisioned a creature as mysterious and ethereal as her name. To help the children focus their listening we designed several sessions in which the children made quick pencil sketches of various characters. It was at this point that our art teacher became directly involved in the project.

Grace Beam, our art teacher, had shown a keen interest in the opera project from the very first year we took part in it because she saw it as an effective way to integrate her teaching more fully into the ongoing curriculum in the classroom. She familiarized herself with the story of *The Magic Flute,* talked with us about our plans and what her role might be in them, and then looked at her art curriculum to see how she could adapt it to accommodate the opera project.

That first year she decided on two projects: The older students would take their pencil sketches and, using the best materials she could provide, turn those sketches into huge tempera paintings of their impressions of scenes from the opera. The younger children would work with sculpture creating magic flutes and magic bells. Since Grace wanted the children to have an extended period of time to involve themselves deeply in their artwork, and since art periods for our students usually run back-to-back, she decided to experiment with some creative scheduling by having the groups alternate weeks. One week the older group skipped art entirely and the younger group had a double session. The following week the younger students remained in the room and the older students had a double art period. It was a great success and our room was soon filled with mysterious Queens of the Night, whimsical birdmen, fierce dragons, beautiful princesses, and handsome princes. We were literally becoming immersed in *The Magic Flute!*

Story Through Dance

Art experiences helped our students understand that one could tell a story using visual means. A combination of music and movement was another avenue we wanted to explore, so we began to work with excerpts from Walt Disney's *Fantasia*, first focusing on the segments at the beginning of the movie in which the artists simply tried to visualize the shapes and colors the music suggested. Then we moved to the vignettes of story images suggested by Tchaikovsky's *Nutcracker Suite*, or Ponchielli's *Dance of the Hours* (with its marvelously ridiculous ostriches and elephants). And finally, we watched the complete story developed from Beethoven's Sixth Symphony (*The Pastoral*).

Movement during this time also had a more directed focus. In order to help children sharpen comprehension skills and to help them learn to interpret the mood of music we asked them to improvise choreography for *Peter and the Wolf*. One can find countless versions of this children's classic, but the one we particularly like is listed in the Annotated Bibliography. It features Claudio Abbado conducting and Sting narrating.

We first listened to the entire piece simply for enjoyment of the story and to absorb the mood of the music. In the next session we played the piece again, stopping to identify each instrument and discussing why a particular instrument was chosen to represent a particular character. During the third session we asked the children to think about which character's movements they would like to choreograph. We aren't sticklers for form. If there are several children who want to be Peter, so be it. Two complete casts leaves plenty of room for choice and solves the problem of finding the space to perform. Each cast has the opportunity of performing and of acting as an audience. The interpretive movement is totally improvisational, challenging the dancers to use expressive body movement to tell the story. It is also excellent practice in sharpening listening skills since each set of characters has to know when to come in. As with every other experience with the fine arts that we offer to the children, we are aware that not every child is going to find dramatic dance his or her forte, but it is one more opportunity for all the children to stretch their interpretive skills and for some to discover a gift for expression they didn't know they possessed.

At this point in the year our students have explored dance and visual arts as a means of telling a story. They had heard stories read aloud and, on those occasions when we were very lucky, they had had the increasingly rare opportunity of being held in the grasp of a live storyteller. They had begun to explore the idea of telling a story through song when they created mini-operas set to familiar melodies. Now the idea of writing their own opera and composing their own original music became one more interesting world of storytelling to explore.

Create and Produce

Their senses heightened by their many experiences with video, storytelling, art, music, and dance, the children were ready for the final stage of the project: the creation of their own opera. There was a strong sense of purpose as we began the work of choosing a book upon which to base the opera. Finding just the right book proved difficult because the children have so many favorites. Fortunately there were practical considerations that helped us focus our thinking:

1. The book had to be inviting enough to engage our audience.
2. It had to contain a story that could involve our entire class.
3. It had to be short enough to enable us to create and produce our opera in the six weeks the music mentor would be with us.

There was a lot of good talk about various stories that might make an interesting opera, but after a great deal of deliberation and negotiation we all agreed that the story for this opera would be *Wind Says Goodnight* written by Katy Rydell and illustrated by David Jorgensen. It is a charming story of a child who can't fall asleep because the mockingbirds are singing too loudly. The wind obligingly asks the mockingbirds to stop singing so the child can go to sleep, but they respond that they can't stop singing until the crickets stop fiddling. When the moon asks the crickets to stop fiddling, they respond that they can't stop playing until the frogs stop strumming. The frogs can't stop strumming until the moths stop dancing. The moths won't stop dancing because the moon is shining so brightly. Finally the wind asks the clouds to cover the moon and bring the rain, and the child finally falls asleep. The whole "It's not my fault" nature of the story was one thing that appealed to our young students. Equally appealing was the fact that characters such as crickets, frogs, moths, clouds, and raindrops would allow them to explore many different types of music from jazz to hoedowns to waltzes.

For the next six weeks we worked as composers, librettists, and choreographers. The phrase "What if . . ." was often heard in our class meetings. From the outset, one of the things that had attracted us to the Cleveland Opera

Project was the emphasis on process. The coordinators both at Opera America and Cleveland Opera were very clear that the "Create and Produce" segment of the project was not to be turned into an extravaganza that would become the school spring program. Emphasis was to be on the process of experiencing the many aspects of producing an opera. The concern shared both by project coordinators and by us as teachers committed to discovery learning was that if schools participating in the project began to think of "Create and Produce" as a performance, adults would feel enormous pressure to take over, and ownership, as well as the sheer joy of mucking about in the world of opera, would be denied to the children. Project developers did expect a performance as a way of synthesizing our work, but it was to be of the workshop variety: low-key, in an intimate setting, meant for a small audience.

As questions generated other questions, threatening to inundate us, we realized that many of the questions arising from our discussions were interrelated. For example, there was the question of how we could include all of our students in some on-stage performance aspect of the opera. With a class of forty-six students that challenge appeared daunting until we thought about it in relation to our question of what to do about sets. We understood the visual impact of scenery, but with a limited amount of time to devote to "Create and Produce," we didn't want to spend a lot of class time making costumes and background scenery.

We solved the problem of elaborate sets by deciding that clouds, rain, moon, and wind in our opera would all be played by children. Instead of one child for each character, we formed character groups, following the same selection process we used for mini-operas. Several children playing the same character also solved another problem: The individual voices of young children are often small and performing on stage, even in a workshop performance, can be daunting. Having the children form character groups strengthens the singing voices and provides the added security a shy child might need in order to perform in front of an audience.

To begin thinking about dialogue for their characters we used a technique originated by Lissy Gulick, one of our former music mentors. The children pretended to sneak up on their characters and listen to their conversation. Keeping the story in mind they asked themselves, "What might the Frogs be talking about? What kind of conversation are the Clouds having? What do you think the Rain is discussing?" Delighted with the opportunity of engaging in sanctioned eavesdropping, the groups generated lively dialogue. As the children conversed, one child acted as a recorder and wrote down everything being said. In those groups where there wasn't a child whose writing skills were developed enough to record the conversation quickly we taped the initial sessions and transcribed them later. The conversation that follows is a transcript of our Cloud group's initial session. As you can see, their conversation was not so much a dialogue as it is a series of questions. Although the list seems endless I have included all of it to illustrate the importance of letting the conversation flow in those first dialogue sessions. You never know where the nugget for a song might be buried.

Clouds

Who's the brightest cloud?
Who's the shortest cloud?
Who's the best cloud?
Who's the loghtest [lightest] cloud?
Who's the littlest cloud?
Who's the happiest cloud?
What are those kids playing?
Who's the happiest cloud?
Who's the misrbalest [miserablest] cloud?
What do animals and humas [humans] feel like?
Who's the scariest cloud?
Who's the darkest cloud?
Are we going to rain or snow?
Who's the thickest cloud?
Who's the longest cloud?
Who's the strongest cloud?
What's the tepature [temperature]?
What's the tepature [temperature] going to be in the morning?
Are we going to be the morning fog?
What kind of cloud am I?
What do I look like?
Who's the bigest [biggest] cloud?
Who's the fluffyest [fluffiest] cloud?
Who's the strongest cloud?
What's that?

In discussing this list of questions the children in the Cloud group made several interesting and important discoveries. They decided that whatever the words to their song turned out to be, they knew that they wanted their music to convey the idea of wonder. And as we read through the long list of questions we realized that tucked near the end of the list were two lines that became the beginning of their song:

What kind of clouds are we?
What do we look like?

Had the adults cut that initial rambling conversation short we would never have gotten to those two questions and would have lost the origin of what turned into a gem of a song set to mysterious, rolling music composed in a minor key.

Cloud Song

What kinds of clouds are we?
What do we look like?
Are we dark?
Are we fluffy?
Are we going to rain,
Or are we going to snow?
Are we going to be the morning fog?
Or will we just drift away and disappear?

And then in response to the Night Wind came the second verse:

Cloud Song

We will cover the earth,
if you carry us.
The moon will hide from us,
if you carry us.
We will cover the moon with
a white, silky blanket
so it will go to sleep,
if you carry us.
Then the rain will come.

When you read the final draft of the Cloud Song it is clear that all of the "messing about" with dialogue and the previous work with writing poetry has provided a foundation upon which these students can build. They are comfortable with imagistic language and they use poetic devices such as a repeated phrase very effectively to create a very lyrical piece that captures the mood perfectly.

Our opera was beginning to take shape. As we moved through the stages of creating characters, choosing roles, writing lyrics, and composing music we made some fundamental discoveries about ourselves and our learning. The cooperative efforts that were so much a part of our students' familiar learning environment translated well to the relatively unfamiliar territory of creating lyrics and music for opera. It was fascinating to observe the children as they worked in small groups fine-tuning the dialogue, choosing and discarding words, negotiating with each other and with the adults until they had a song that captured the essence of their character. The journey was not always a smooth one and our students learned some difficult lessons about give-and-take. Our Cricket group, for example, put a lot of effort into developing the following song:

Crickets

We can fiddle faster than you.
No, you can't.
Oh, yes, we can.
No, you can't.
Yes, we can. We're the best fiddlers in the world.
I guess we need fiddling lessons.
We can teach you how to fiddle.

In response to the Night Wind's request to stop fiddling:

We don't want to stop
'Cause we're having too much fun.
We just got fiddling lessons.
Frogs' strumming makes our fiddling sound good.
Tell the Frogs to stop strumming then we'll stop fiddling.

It was a good song, but once we tried it with the rest of the story it became clear that the first verse didn't fit. The song needed to be reworked so that it kept the essence of the fun of fiddling but stayed within the story line. There was a lot of initial grumbling and resistance on the part of the Cricket group. After all, they had invested tremendous effort in their song and they had worked well together. Once they were allowed to vent their disappointment they were able to see that they were responsible not only to their small collaborative group, but also to the creation and success of the entire opera. It is during this type of revision that an adult mentor, be it teacher, parent helper, or music mentor, is so important because this is where the adult can "take off the top of her head," as Nancie Atwell likes to say, and model the kinds of revision techniques and collaborative skills the children need to move forward. The creation of opera provides many such teaching opportunities. Our Crickets ended up with a show-stopping hoedown piece that had the audience clapping and stamping:

Crickets

(Chirp low, then high, four times to find the right beat)
Proud to be crickets.
Playing our fiddles.
Fiddling high . . . *(fiddle music)*
Fiddling low . . . *(fiddle music)*
Fiddling to the dance of the do-si-do.
(Chirps, same rhythm as above)
Proud to be crickets.
Playing our fiddles.
Fiddling fast.
Fiddling slow.
Fiddling to the dance of the do-si-do.
(Hoedown fiddle music)

After the Night Wind asks them to stop playing:

Crickets

We don't want to stop
'Cause we're having too much fun.
The frogs strumming
Makes our fiddling sound good.
Tell the frogs to stop strumming,
Then we'll stop fiddling . . . fiddling . . . fiddling.

Creative thinking flourished and language arts skills such as comprehension of main ideas, sequence, sentence structure, drafting, revision, and editing were developing continually as children wrote the libretto for their opera. Collaborative group skills—part of every school's social studies curriculum—got a constant workout as children were reminded to think of how their particular piece fit into the whole. These are valuable skills and opera provided a motivating framework that kept our kids engaged.

Working as Composers

Our confidence buoyed by the shared experience of creating songs from dialogue, we were ready to work on the composition of music for our lyrics, and on the staging of our opera for a workshop performance in front of an audience of parents and relatives. For teachers with no formal musical training, composing music is still the most intimidating phase of the opera project, but it always turns out to be a true learning experience for all involved. It is during "Create and Produce" that the Cleveland Opera provides a music mentor who meets with the class for ten one-hour sessions. Each new mentor is interested in knowing what has gone on before, and then adds new techniques to our teaching repertoire, expanding our understanding of the process. When our most recent opera mentor Chas Smith arrived, for example, we shared with him the way Lissy had managed to demystify the process of composing, making it accessible to novices. She had helped us visualize whole notes, for example, by explaining them as rubber bands that have to be stretched out. She had asked various children to read lines from a song so that we could all hear where the voice naturally pitched high and low and where emphasis was placed. Those highs and lows became notes on a staff.

Chas incorporated many of those techniques into his sessions and added some of his own. He would often ask several different children to sing part of a song so he could capture the mood. Then he would translate what he heard to the keyboard. He always knew when he *got it* because the kids would literally light up! Once a line was composed Chas would ask the children to sing that line and then keep singing into the next line to see where the melody would go. This was a particularly effective technique and our students found it easy to follow the music wherever it wanted to go because of all their experiences with music and movement. As we watched them work through this process we couldn't help reflecting on other times encounters with the arts had allowed our students to hear this message from mentors: potter Chris Breuer talking about how he had to listen to the clay, music teacher Joanne Erwin's students demonstrating the way members of a string quartet must listen to each other in order for the piece to work, poet Debra Chandra talking about why it is important to "follow a poem wherever it wants to go." These people were not only teaching children about art; they were teaching them about life.

Chas fully understood our emphasis on student ownership and would always ask the class to choose from several alternatives. Rhythm really sets the mood for a piece, and there were times when we adults had one mood in mind and the children had a very different idea. Sometimes the music they wanted to compose seemed to be a complete departure from the mood of the rest of the opera. We often had our reservations, but we knew from past experience that even though it might take some time for them to get there, the children's instincts were usually right on target. In every case they created melodies that were perfect for their characters. It was hard at times to keep from offering unneeded advice, but we knew our students appreciated the respect adults were showing for their judgment. It was also beneficial for the children to realize that all of us were starting out at the same point in this composing business, and they benefited from watching their teachers work through a new learning process right in front of them.

"Create and Produce" provided many new learning experiences for us within the classroom, but it also allowed us to extend our classroom community beyond the walls of the school. The design of the project originally called for only one opera professional to act as music mentor. It wasn't long, however, before the excitement and infectious spirit of our endeavor drew in some of our parents who had expertise to offer.

One parent, a librarian by profession, was so excited by the opera workshop that she spent several of her days off sharing the expertise she had developed as a member of a community choral group. Her infectious spirit provided a tremendous sense of energy to the Cricket group with whom she worked. Another parent offered to be the fiddler for our Cricket group and his hoedown music added a special dimension to our opera. Still another parent, interested in theater, offered to work with the Night Wind. Our music teacher decided that music class for our children would be a good time to compose the Moth song, with all the children contributing ideas to the group. Whenever the LD teacher came to work with students in our room she got involved in the project as well. During any given composing session Chas might be working with two or three groups, we would each take a group, and one of the parents would have a group. It kept the sessions small and made it much easier for children to participate fully. Anyone walking into the room could literally feel and hear the hum of energy being produced by this unique team of children, professionals, and volunteers.

During the six weeks of "Create and Produce" the entire curriculum was framed by the study of music and the connections children made to the rest of their learning were significant. As we worked and reworked melodies, for example, choosing, rearranging, and discarding, several children commented that what they were doing was "just like the rough drafts we do in writing." As adults we had been struck by the close parallels between drafting and composing, but it was the playing with words and music that allowed the children to make those same discoveries. That type of connection was proof to us that the opera project was providing an environment where learning was taking place on many levels.

Students also honed reading and writing skills as they composed the libretto, and stretched into new areas as they read and wrote myths. The study of opera is an excellent time to introduce the genre of the myth and we found that after sharing a book such as *How Music Came to the World,* retold by Hal Ober and illustrated by Carol Ober, the children were excited about writing their own versions of the story. The type of thinking and the skills developed in creating the opera libretto allowed words to flow easily, helping students to internalize the feel, form, and language of the myth.

Reading choices during the weeks of opera workshop ranged from biographies of musicians and dancers to informational books about musical instruments and the scientific study of sound. Our students used these nonfiction books as resources when exploring science investigations involving the study of sound waves through work with oscilloscope patterns, experiments that involve the study of the human ear, and an investigation of timbre as it relates to musical instruments.

They also used them during the research element of the workshop. Children studied families of instruments, learned the characteristics by which to categorize them, and then explored our nonfiction offerings to find a simple instrument they would like to build. Students were to find the instrument they wanted to build, record directions for building it, and then gather simple materials to construct their instruments at school. It is a project broad enough to fit the needs of children all along the spectrum of development. Students just beginning to develop as readers and writers often choose an uncomplicated project, such as using a spaghetti box and rubber bands to create a simple violin. More advanced students choose more complex projects that involve several steps. These more advanced projects often involve collaborative work with a partner, and it is interesting to see how such partner pairs plan their time and divide the work. And because the research project is so open-ended, it allows full reign to a student like Alex, who chose to research and build an instrument that was a challenge for his unique skills (see Figure 6.1).

At the same time they are researching and building instruments our students were learning to compose original pieces of music. Building on research

■ FIGURE 6.1 Alex's directions for a zither

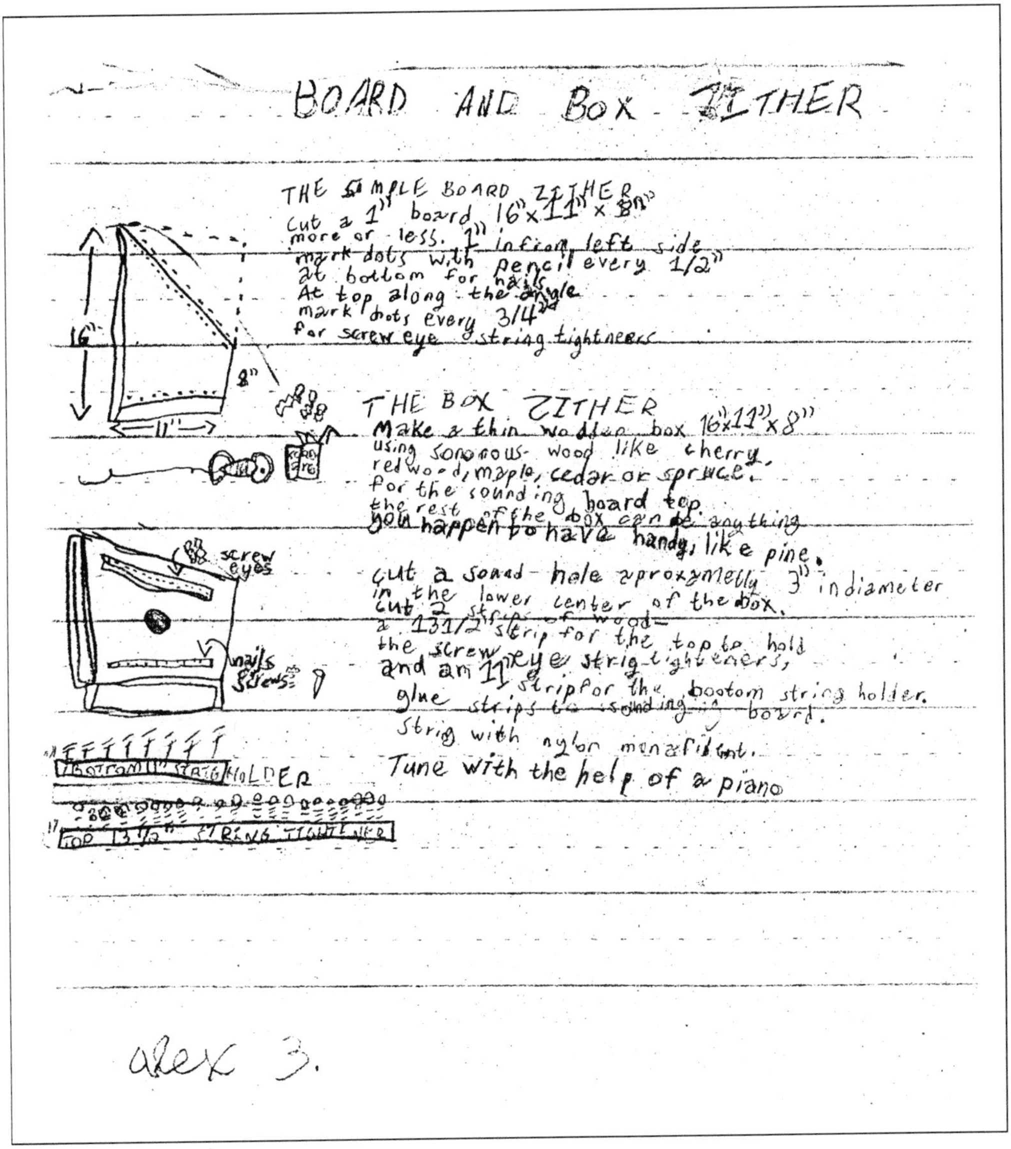

Alex 3.

done by our colleague Ray Levi, and on the work of Rena Upitis, author of *Can I Play You My Song?*, we encouraged the children to use invented composition just as they use functional spelling in writing to get their musical ideas down on paper. We asked them to follow Rena Upitis's simple rules, which we paraphrase here.

1. Work with a partner.
2. Choose two different instruments.
3. Use blank paper and find a way to record your song so that someone else will be able to play it without your guidance.

As you can see from the examples in Figures 6.2 and 6.3 the recording methods children used were quite different. What was important to us as teachers was how easily our students saw the parallels between invented composition and functional spelling, and that invented composition was

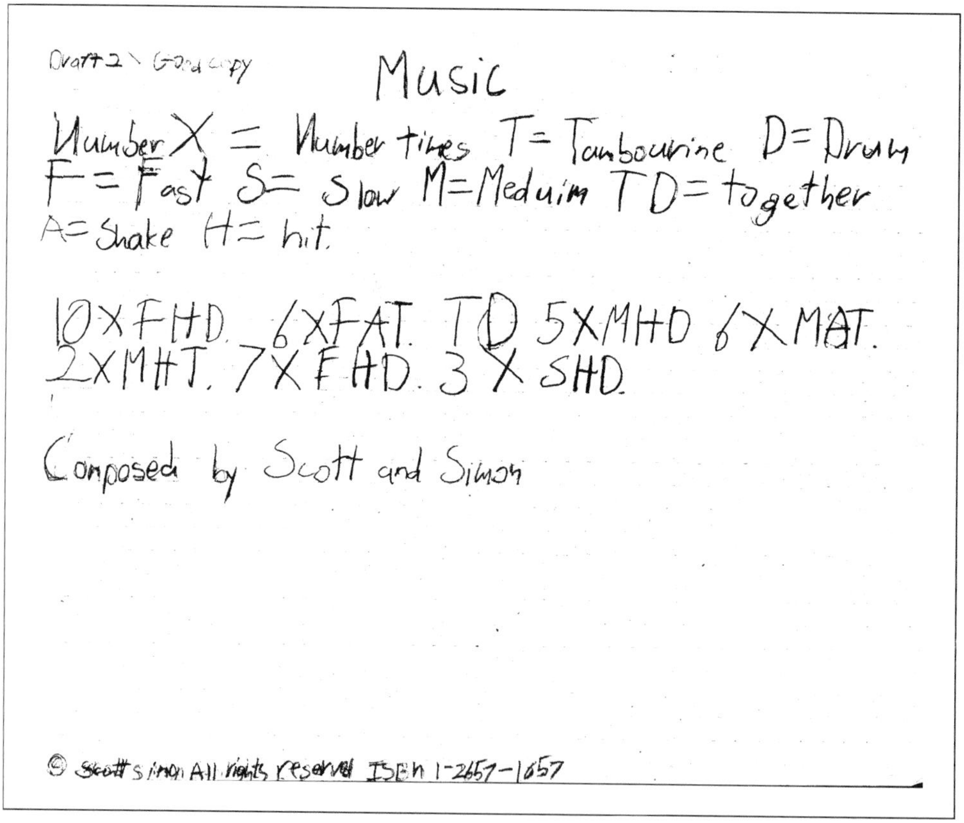
Draft 2 \ Good copy

Music

Number X = Number times T= Tambourine D= Drum
F= Fast S= Slow M=Meduim TD= together
A= Shake H= hit.

10XFHD. 6XFAT. TD 5XMHD 6XMAT.
2XMHT. 7XFHD. 3X SHD.

Composed by Scott and Simon

© Scott Simon All rights reserved ISBN 1-2657-1657

■ **FIGURE 6.2 Scott and Simon's invented composition**

▪ **FIGURE 6.3 Ian and Alice's invented composition**

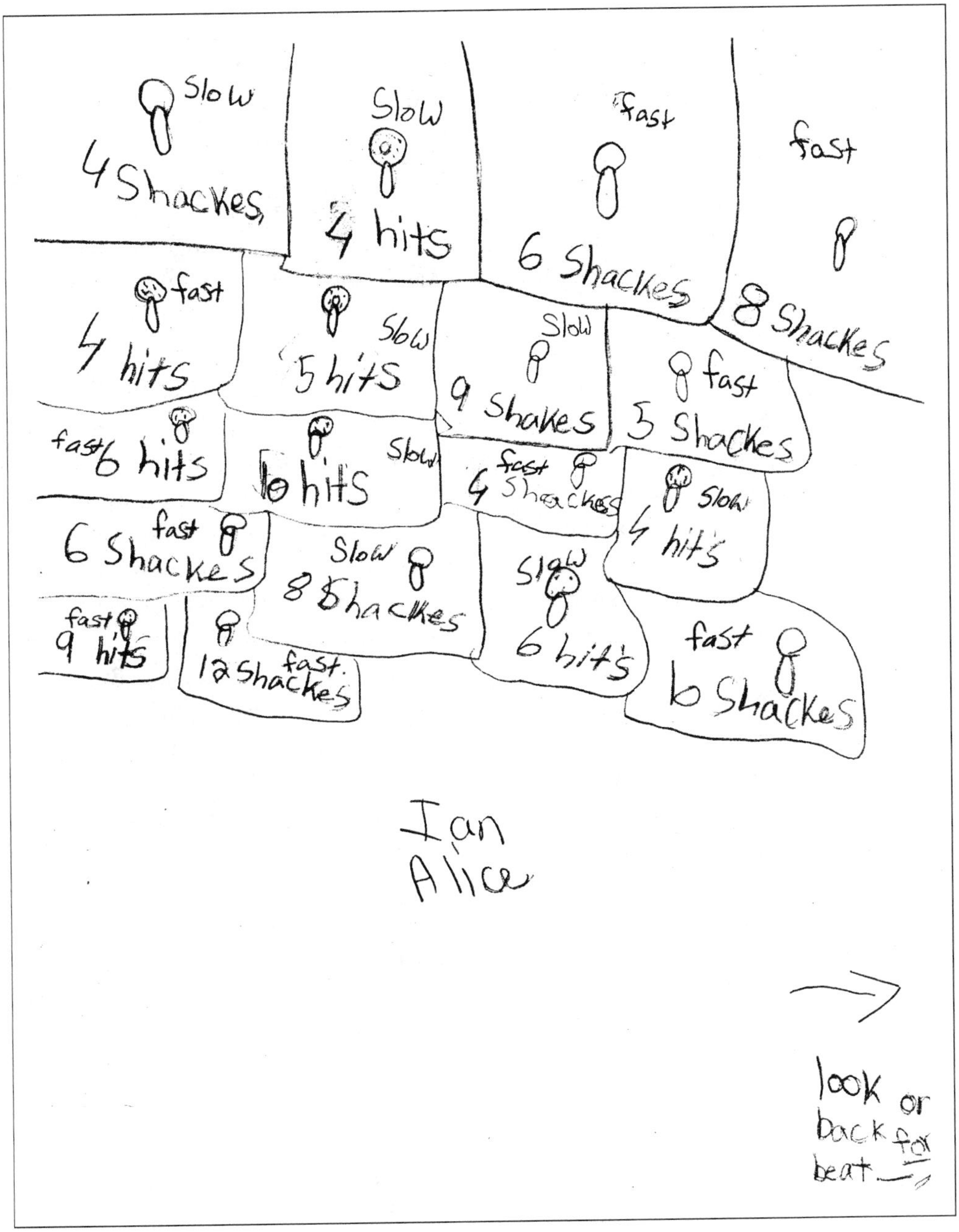

another way they could communicate ideas. This is an exciting new area for us and we will be pursuing work with invented composition as an ongoing project.

"Create and Produce" is often a time that causes us to reflect upon our teaching philosophy. Process oriented though we may be, we sometimes found a familiar and unsettling phenomenon developing as we approached the date of the performance. Whenever that situation begins to descend on us we remember an incident that occurred the first time we took part in *MUSIC! WORDS! OPERA!*

It was two days before the performance. With some songs still to be set to music and choreography changing almost daily as people were struck with new interpretations, everyone began to sense a tension that hadn't existed before. Suddenly the concept of the importance of the *process* was being overwhelmed by the pressure to finish things. The news that both the major funders of the project and the director of Cleveland Opera were going to be in the audience created an almost overwhelming desire to turn our workshop into a polished performance. We were torn between our commitment to discovery learning and the desire to have the audience understand that our time had been well spent.

Judith Ryder, director of Cleveland Opera On Tour, and Lissy, our mentor that year, were discussing with us the songs that still needed music. We adults were feeling a little desperate at the prospect of all that still had to be done when Sarah, the second grader who played our Moon, said very quietly, "I don't think I want my song set to music. It is so sad that it feels right just to speak it softly." The confidence in that child's voice and the self-assurance that four adult professionals would respect her decision acted like a magnet to pull us back to our original purpose. This project was not about an opera performance for an audience—it was about joy and wonder, discovery and connections, celebration and community. And most of all, it was about children taking charge of their learning. It is a memory that snaps us out of our panic every time.

Our latest experience with opera workshop produced some surprises of its own. One evening a few days before the performance found us involved in an experiment that resulted when several events came together. Over the past few years of the project our art teacher has looked for opportunities to expand her role, experimenting with ways to provide different experiences for the children. This past year, for example, she worked with our students to design a background scene for *Wind Says Goodnight*. The integration of art and language arts was clear as she worked with the children retelling the story in order to identify elements that would be a part of the scenic background.

Once those elements were agreed upon they made pencil sketches which they shared, discussed, and then used to create a huge six-by-eighteen-foot mural that would become the background scene for the performance.

The children had also been thinking about making some simple props and costumes. They had spent time making quick sketches of what their costumes might look like. We wanted to honor their wishes for costumes and simple sets, but as we said earlier in the chapter we did not want to use blocks of valuable "Create and Produce" time to do it. A conversation with another teacher in the county who was taking part in the opera project provided the inspiration for our experiment. We decided to have a *Family Fun Night*.

We picked an evening three days before the performance and invited all families to come to the gym to help make simple costumes and paint the background scene Grace had sketched with the children. We laid down plastic, set out paint, brushes, and sponges, and let parents and children go to work painting the penciled sketch.

In other parts of the gym parents and children were designing frog costumes, bird costumes, and bass fiddles for the frogs. The room was filled with a busy hum and high spirits of children and adults completely engrossed in their work. In a two-hour time period the background scene was completed and we had costumes and props for all of the characters in the opera.

These days when time for families is so short it was very satisfying to see parents and kids in a completely relaxed situation enjoying being together, and we realized that such moments are one of the quieter benefits of this opera project. Of course there were disappointments. The turnout was small (about twelve families) and some of the families we most wanted to reach did not come, but we know that next time we need to make a more concerted effort to reach those families. We don't expect a 100 percent turnout, but after witnessing the warm exchanges between parents and kids we want more of our families to have the opportunity of spending that kind of time together.

The night of the performance finally arrived and the atmosphere in the gym was alive with anticipation as Chas played a short overture and excited children took their places for the beginning of the opera. From the moment those bright-feathered Mockingbirds began their raucous opening song, to the dreamy waltz of the moon-stricken Moths, to the ethereal Clouds who finally saved the day by covering up the Moon's glow, the audience was completely caught up in the opera. They commiserated with the poor children who were trying to sleep and swayed along with the Night Wind as it glided in and out of the story, carrying the children's message to each unheeding character. Toes tapped and hands clapped as the Crickets played and sang their hoedown music, and when the Frogs swaggered onstage with their bass fiddles, sunglasses adding the perfect touch to their cool image and jazzy, bluesy music, the audience really *got down* with them!

As we watched from the front row we were struck once again by the power of the arts to widen the learning circle. Several of the Moth characters, quiet children when it came to speaking, danced with a fluid grace. A visually impaired child, safely tucked between two classmates, sang with gusto. A child with a severe hearing impairment, and a hyperactive child, for whom academic growth had been a real challenge, were difficult to spot in that group of Frogs.

And then there was Sam, who as late as the afternoon of the performance was saying, "I can't do it. I'll be too scared." As he waited nervously for his part of the Rain we held our breath, hoping that our reassurances had had the desired effect, but knowing that it was just as likely he would opt out at the last minute. The Rain music began, Sam looked out at the audience, and an amazing transformation took place as he stomped onstage, the best thunder rain we had ever seen. The real moment came when his group finished their song and Sam flashing a huge grin, announced in a stage whisper, "That was fun!"

The audience responded with a standing ovation, struck by the fact that these young children had written such poetic lyrics, composed music that so perfectly captured the essence of each character, and performed with such joy and confidence. That confidence was born of the fact that these children hadn't been playing at being composers and lyricists and dancers; they *were* composers, lyricists, and dancers. They didn't have to worry about memorizing someone else's lines; they had lived with the words of their songs through one draft after another until those words were a part of them. Our brother and sister team of Kara and A. J. spoke for all of us with what they wrote in their self-evaluations. Kara said, "music can make you feel differen ways. it can make you Happy sad and mad and scared. Music can make you Feel like all sorts of things." A. J. completed the thought with one sentence: "I lerd tet wen you sert an opra you cannt stop." (I learned that when you start an opera you can't stop.)

Thinking about opera didn't stop with the performance. After a reading of *Swan Lake* Micah realized that Siegfried fell in love with the swan Odette as quickly as Tamino fell in love with Pamina in *The Magic Flute*. "It's just like Tamino looking at the picture of Pamina!" he exclaimed. Because our study of *The Magic Flute* had given us a common language, everyone in the class knew what Micah was talking about. This common language, this knowledge of opera as a form of human expression, helped engender a genuine sense of classroom community.

The opera project also brought unexpected and rich encounters. One of the most memorable came about after our first opera experience and involved a decision to write to the author and illustrator of the book we had turned into an opera. The children's letters always provide insight into their understanding of their work with opera, but sometimes those letters are also the cause of events none of us could have predicted. Their letters to William Stafford and Debra Frasier, author and illustrator respectively, of the book *The Animal That Drank Up Sound,* were just such an event and the beginning of a very special relationship. This was the book that we had adapted for our first experience with the opera project. Both writer and illustrator were overwhelmed that children had honored their work, and told them so in a series of letters. Here are some of William Stafford's words:

> Meeting you at NCTE was a great bonus; and by now I have basked in the packet of materials you kindly turned over to me. What a wonderful project it all is! In the words of Micah Mitchell, I found much to rejoice in, "a strange feeling in my heart and I wish I had that feeling all the time." All the papers gave me a feeling I wish I had all the time, and I am grateful to the students and to you for letting this writer know how a book can reach out.

And this is part of Debra Frasier's response:

> It is a lot of work to shepherd a book into the world, but the unexpected ways it winds its way into the most surprising places (imagine: an opera springs up in Ohio! Who would ever thought?) is wonderful and amazing, and unlike anything else I know.

It was heartwarming for the children to hear Debra's response, and tremendously exciting to have a poet the stature of William Stafford so touched by the children's work. The sad fact that this wonderful man died not long after our initial opera project made our letter exchange that much more special.

Our immersion in the world of music and opera had lasting effects on us as a community. Because we had been willing to take risks and follow our collective vision, we had shared an experience full of creativity and wonderment. As the poet W. B. Yeats once said, "Art bids us touch and taste and hear and see the world."

We responded to that bidding.

Epilogue: Insights and Inquiries

The central thesis proposed at the beginning of this book was that by extending the definition of *language* to include music, dance, poetry, and the visual arts we could widen the learning circle and engage more children in more satisfying ways. We've painted a detailed picture of the environments we construct with children so that you might have a map with which to follow our journey as we weave the individual threads of the arts into the fabric of the classroom curriculum. As we look back we see those threads developing into interesting patterns that have led to some valuable insights.

One of the most basic and rewarding of those insights is the validation of questions, talk, and listening as central to student learning. Our experience has shown that talk makes all of our thinking bigger by encouraging self-reflection and by supporting the belief that knowledge shared is knowledge enhanced. When students are encouraged to articulate their understandings about learning they are on firmer footing and more willing to take the risks needed to move on. Talk becomes the scaffold upon which to stand in order to reach the next level of understanding.

One cannot focus on the importance of talk and questions without also focusing on the importance of listening as a component of all that talk. Listening is not an innate skill, and if we are to enlarge the role of talk in our daily curriculum and gain some sense of ease with the amount of time such an effort requires during the teaching day, then we have to train ourselves to listen differently.

This new slant on talking and listening is a lot easier to write about than it is to practice. It is hard work, especially in the beginning. It is difficult to ignore the nagging thought that we should be *teaching*. But the more we allow students the time to develop the ability to speak in articulate ways the more we realize how the rest of the curriculum is enhanced when talk is treated as the catalyst that drives learning. We *are* teaching when we spend precious classroom time developing speaking and listening skills.

Another insight that came out of our work is that as the learning circle was being widened and deepened walls of all kinds were beginning to disappear. Divisions between disciplines began to blur as children looked at learning from multiple perspectives. Nowhere is this more obvious than in our immersion workshops. These workshops provide the opportunity for students to synthesize much of what they have gleaned from the models and mentors with whom they have worked, and encourage them to see the connections between disciplines so that they enlarge their own thinking and extend the possibilities for learning.

This practice of *bridging,* using experiences from one learning situation and discipline to think about concepts in another discipline, enhances the learning of all of our students, but appears to be crucial to the growth of students who are struggling with the traditional reading/writing/thinking approach of traditional classrooms. These students not only appear to thrive because there is a place for their preferred style of learning, but also seem to be using that preferred modality, e.g., drawing, as a way to access and understand the more traditional sign systems. Is this because the infusion of the fine arts into the daily curriculum more closely resembles the multiple ways children approach learning with all of their senses before they began formal schooling, and therefore allows them to build on the familiar, to do what comes naturally? We will continue to track this data closely because, if the pattern continues, it has important implications concerning the learning of young children.

The inclusion of the arts into the curriculum also appears to help break down barriers between school and community. When we first began to generate the questions for our research we did not consciously set out to ask the question of how to involve the community more effectively in the school. We had always mined the community for support when the children's interests outstripped our expertise. Knowing that we couldn't be equally proficient in music, dance, poetry, and the visual arts has provided the impetus to invite professionals and devotees of the arts to come and work with us as we explored the idea of looking at the world through multiple lenses. When they could physically be present that was wonderful: when they couldn't, we used audiotapes or videotapes as ways of accessing their thinking. One result of widening the learning circle is that it stretches beyond the boundaries of the building. By broadening the definition of language to include the fine arts we also broadened the opportunities for inviting experts into our classroom to act as models and mentors.

As we look to the future we realize that there are significant challenges to be met. One of these challenges is that of priorities. Teachers involved in whole language classrooms made the discovery early on that students were becoming more accomplished readers and writers because we were designing our classrooms to include significantly more time for students to read and write. If we are now extending the definition of language to include music, dance, poetry, and the visual arts, the assumption follows that children will become more adept at communicating through these domains only if we make space in our curriculum for composing, moving, and sketching. How do we convince those responsible for students' education to see multiliteracy as a priority when a vocal segment of the public is agitating loudly for back-to-basics? How do we help people understand that the arts *are* basic to learning?

Furthermore, if, as a body of research is beginning to show, many students communicate more effectively through the arts, aren't we shortchanging them if we don't explore this exciting possibility for extending student learning? What would such an exploration mean for the way teachers are trained, the way students are taught, and the way classrooms are organized?

What kinds of ongoing support will be provided to help classroom teachers become more comfortable with the arts? What kinds of assessment tools will we need to develop so that we can share progress with parents, administrators, and other interested parties? How will we design assessment criteria so that we are not using old methods to evaluate new approaches?

Programs such as Arts PROPEL and studies such as The Harvard Project Zero Approach to Arts Education have paved the way for investigating new methods of assessment that use multiple measures and are context specific. We need to find out more about such assessment tools so our tests are fair ones. We also need to think about linking Artist-In-Residence programs with ongoing mentorships of classroom teachers so that those teachers who are unfamiliar with the fine arts can build a foundation that will allow them to see the possibilities the arts hold for learning. These are important and exciting challenges to be met.

This particular journey has come to an end, but like all worthwhile journeys it has left us with intriguing questions and tantalizing possibilities to explore further. We approached the writing of this book as the continuation of a dialogue that was first initiated when we began our teaching partnership, a dialogue that grew to include our colleagues who work with us, and through this book widens to include all of you. We hope you will view our words as the beginning of a conversation through which we all continue to explore the possibilities for widening the learning circle.

Appendix A

Open Room Morning Schedule

8:45–9:10
Morning routine: sign in, sign up for read-aloud or literature circle, weather, calendar, and SQUIRT (Sustained Quiet Uninterrupted Reading Time, when children read quietly alone or with a friend).

9:10–9:15
Poetry read-aloud, open room daily schedule

9:15–10:15
Work period: children work at centers on investigations based on current thematic focus. Alternating morning and afternoon work periods, this is also the time when one teacher focuses on reading with her home-base students and the other teacher oversees math investigations and other centers.

Monday, Wednesday, and Friday Mornings

10:15–10:30
Cleanup and recess.

10:30–11:00
Movement or science talk

11:00–12:00
Writing workshop begins with a minilesson (handwriting, spelling, phonics, writing technique, grammar), then moves to workshop in which children work on ongoing writing projects, and ends with a short class share of works in progress.

171

12:10–12:45
Lunch and recess

Tuesday Morning Schedule

10:20–10:55
Music for firsts, language arts for seconds

11:00–11:40
Class meeting

11:40–12:15
Music for seconds, language arts for firsts

12:15–12:55
Lunch and recess

Thursday Morning

10:20–10:55
Music for firsts, language arts for seconds

11:00–11:35
Music for seconds, language arts for firsts

11:35–12:05
Class meeting

12:10–12:45
Lunch and recess

Appendix B

From Fairy Tale to Opera: A Step-by-Step Approach

Step 1. Find time in the day (e.g., as the students arrive in the morning) to play music from ballets or operas based on fairy tales (*Sleeping Beauty, Hansel and Gretel, Swan Lake*).

Step 2. Read fairy tales, folk tales, and nursery rhymes aloud to the class.

Step 3. Use text sets of fairy tales and folk tales for reading instruction.

Step 4. Develop literature circles to retell stories children have been reading. Use journal writing to respond to the stories, focusing on such questions as: How can we tell whether a story is a *Cinderella, Three Little Pigs,* or *Red Riding Hood* story? What kinds of characters do we expect to meet in fairy tales? How does a fairy tale begin? End? What usually happens in a fairy tale?

Step 5. Discuss elements of an opera. View a children's opera live if possible, or on video.

Step 6. Brainstorm a list of fairy tales, folk tales, and nursery rhymes that would make good operas.

Step 7. Children form interest groups based upon which operas they would like to perform.

Step 8. Review a familiar melody (e.g., *Skip to My Lou, London Bridge, Go Tell Aunt Rhody*) to be used as a melody for the mini-opera. Children practice fitting words to a melody by composing a song about a friend and what the friend likes to do. The following song is to *Skip to My Lou.*

Ian likes to play soccer.
Ian likes to play soccer.
Ian likes to play soccer.
And he likes to read books, too.

Step 9. Model the development of one opera (perhaps a nursery rhyme) as a whole group process.

Step 10. Interest groups work on retelling their story to that melody. Words are not written down. They may change (and do) as long as they tell the story and fit the melody.

Step 11. In-process performances for the class. Class learns to critique in a helpful way. Name three things the group did well. Tell them one thing they can do to make their opera better.

Step 12. Invite one or two other classes to watch operas so students will get used to an audience.

Step 13. Perform mini-operas for parents. Mini-operas should be done in the classroom. Minimal attention should be paid to scenery or costumes; it is the *process* that is important.

Appendix C

Thematic Unit Self-Assessment

Arts and Artists

Which project made you feel the proudest?

What project did you feel was the hardest?

What else would you like to learn about artists?

References

Works Cited

Adoff, Arnold. 1979. *Eats*. New York: Lothrop, Lee, and Shepard.

———. 1989. *Chocolate Dreams*. New York: Lothrop, Lee, and Shepard.

———. 1993. "The Poem Singing into Your Eyes." In *Poems That Sing to You*. Ed. Michael Strickland. Honesdale, PA: Boyds Mills Press.

Arnosky, Jim. 1982. *Drawing from Nature*. New York: Lothrop, Lee, and Shepard.

———. 1988a. *Sketching Outdoors in Autumn*. New York: Lothrop, Lee, and Shepard.

———. 1988b. *Sketching Outdoors in Winter*. New York: Lothrop, Lee, and Shepard.

Art Gallery. Microsoft. Cognitive Applications Limited, Brighton, England. CD-ROM.

Atwell, Nancie. 1995. Taking Off the Top of My Head. Paper presented at the Fall Conference of the National Council of Teachers of English, San Diego, CA.

Berry, James. 1996. *Rough Sketch Beginning*. New York: Harcourt Brace.

Bjork, Christina, and Lena Anderson. 1987. *Linnea in Monet's Garden*. New York: Farrar, Straus, and Giroux.

Bohm-Duchen, Monica, and Janet Cook. 1991. *Understanding Modern Art*. London: Usborne Publishing Ltd.

Calkins, Lucy, with Shelley Harwayne. 1991. *Living Between the Lines*. Portsmouth, NH: Heinemann.

Cherry, Lynne. 1992. *A River Ran Wild*. New York: Harcourt Brace Jovanovich.

Clifton, Lucille. 1995. Oberlin College Conference.

Coles, Robert. 1989. *The Call of Stories*. Boston: Houghton Mifflin.

Collins, David R. 1989. *The Country Artist*. Minneapolis: Carolrhoda Books.

Copeland, Jeffrey S. 1993. *Speaking of Poets: Interviews with Poets Who Write for Children and Young Adults*. Urbana, IL: National Council of Teachers of English.

Copeland, Jeffrey S., and Vicky L. Copeland. 1994. *Speaking of Poets 2: More Interviews with Poets Who Write for Children and Young Adults*. Urbana, IL: National Council of Teachers of English.

Corsi, Jerome R. 1995. *Leonardo da Vinci*. Rohnert Park, CA: Pomegranate Artbooks.

Criswell, Susie. 1994. *Nature Through Science and Art*. Blue Ridge Summit, PA: McGraw-Hill.

dePaola, Tomie. 1989. *The Art Lesson*. New York: Trumpet.

———. 1991. *Bonjour, Mr. Satie*. New York: G. P. Putnam.

Disney. 1991. *For Our Children*. Burbank, CA: Disney Press.

Doubilet, Anne. 1991. *Under the Sea from A to Z*. New York: Crown.

Eisner, Elliot W. 1991. *The Enlightened Eye*. New York: Macmillan.

———. 1994a. *Cognition and Curriculum Reconsidered*. 2d ed. New York: Teachers College Press.

———. 1994b. Conference on English Leadership speech. Paper presented at the Fall Conference of the National Council of Teachers of English, Orlando, FL.

Eisner, Elliot, and Alan Peshkin, eds. 1990. *Qualitative Inquiry in Education: The Continuing Debate*. New York: Teachers College Press.

Elting, Mary, and Michael Folsom. 1980. *Q Is for Duck*. New York: Clarion.

Ernst, Karen. 1994. *Picturing Learning*. Portsmouth, NH: Heinemann.

Feelings, Tom, ed. 1993. *Soul Looks Back in Wonder*. New York: Dial.

Fletcher, Ralph. 1991. *Water Planet*. Paramus, NJ: Arrowhead Books.

Fleischman, Paul. 1988. *Joyful Noise: Poems for Two Voices*. New York: Harper and Row.

Fowler, Charles, and OPERA America. 1990. *MUSIC! WORDS! OPERA! Level I Teacher's Manual*. Washington, DC: MMB Music.

Fox, Mem. 1985. *Wilfred Gordon MacDonald Partridge*. New York: Kane/Miller.

Fraser, Jane, and Donna Skolnick. 1994. *On Their Way: Celebrating Second Graders as They Read and Write*. Portsmouth, NH: Heinemann.

Gallas, Karen. 1995. *Talking Their Way into Science: Hearing Children's Questions and Theories, Responding with Curricula*. New York: Teachers College Press.

Gardner, Howard. 1980. *Artful Scribbles: The Significance of Children's Drawings*. New York: Basic.

———. 1991. *The Unschooled Mind: How Children Think and How Schools Should Teach*. New York: Basic.

———. 1993. *Creating Minds*. New York: Basic.

George, Jean Craighead. 1993. *Dear Rebecca, Winter Is Here*. New York: HarperCollins.

Grallert, Margot. 1992. "Working from the Inside Out: A Practical Approach to Expression." In *Arts as Education*. Ed. Meryl Ruth Goldberg and Ann Phillips. Cambridge: Harvard Educational Review.

Graves, Donald H. 1989. *Investigate Nonfiction*. Portsmouth, NH: Heinemann.

Gray, Libba Moore. 1995. *My Mama Had a Dancing Heart*. New York: Orchard.

Greene, Maxine. 1992. "Texts and Margins." In *Arts as Education*. Ed. Meryl Ruth Goldberg and Ann Phillips. Cambridge: Harvard Educational Review.

Greenfield, Eloise. 1978. *Honey, I Love and Other Love Poems*. New York: Thomas Y. Crowell.

Grooms, Red. 1988. *Ruckus Rodeo*. New York: Harry N. Abrams.

Heard, Georgia. 1992. *Creatures of Earth, Sea, and Sky*. Honesdale, PA: Boyds Mills Press.

Hughes, Langston. 1995. *The Book of Rhythms.* New York: Oxford University Press.

Hulme, Joy N. 1993. *What If? Just Wondering Poems.* Honesdale, PA: Boyds Mills Press.

Janeczko, Paul, ed. 1994. *Poetry from A to Z.* New York: Bradbury.

Joyes, Claire. 1989. *Monet's Table: Cooking Journals of Claude Monet.* New York: Simon and Schuster.

Kirby, Dan, and Carol Kuykendall. 1991. *Mind Matters: Teaching for Thinking.* Portsmouth, NH: Boynton/Cook.

Kitchen, Bert. 1992. *Somewhere Today.* Cambridge: Candlewick Press.

Kulling, Monica. 1994. "New Mexico Music." *Cricket,* March, 30.

Landau, Diana, ed. 1991. *In Nature's Heart: The Wilderness Days of John Muir.* San Francisco: Walking Stick Press.

Lanker, Brian. 1989. *I Dream a World: Portraits of Black Women Who Changed America.* New York: Stewart, Tabori, and Chang.

Lecourt, Nancy. 1991. *Abracadabra to Zigzag.* New York: Lothrop, Lee, and Shepard Books.

Lewis, Richard. 1988. "Bridges Between Formal and Informal Education." Cleveland, OH: Cleveland Children's Museum.

Lionni, Leo. 1967. *Frederick.* New York: Pantheon.

Lipman, Jean, with Margaret Aspinwall. 1981. *Alexander Calder and His Magical Mobiles.* New York: Hudson Hills Press.

Locker, Thomas. 1995. *Sky Tree: Seeing Science Through Art.* New York: HarperCollins.

Lyon, George Ella. 1989. *Together.* New York: Orchard.

———. 1992. *Who Came Down That Road?* New York: Orchard.

Madoff, Steven. 21 January 1996. "Art in Cyberspace: Can It Live Without a Body?" *New York Times,* 1, 34–35.

Mahy, Margaret. 1987. *17 Kings and 42 Elephants.* New York: Dial.

Marshall, Edward (James). 1981. *Three by the Sea.* New York: Dial.

Martin, Bill Jr., and John Archambault. 1989. *Chicka Chicka Boom Boom.* New York: Simon and Schuster.

Mayers, Florence Cassen. 1988. *ABC Musical Instruments from the Metropolitan Museum of Art.* New York: Harry N. Abrams.

Merriam, Eve. 1993. "Umbilical." In *Poems That Sing to You.* Ed. Michael Strickland. Honesdale, PA: Boyds Mills Press.

Moffitt, John. 1966. "To Look at Any Thing." In *Reflections on a Gift of Watermelon Pickle and Other Modern Verse.* Ed. Stephen Dunning, Edward Lueders, and Hugh Smith. Glenview, IL: Scott Foresman.

Moore, Bill. 1987. *Words That Taste Good.* Markham, Ontario: Pembroke.

Moore, Lillian. 1988. *I'll Meet You at the Cucumbers.* New York: Atheneum.

Morgan, Genevieve, ed. 1996. *Monet: The Artist Speaks.* San Francisco: HarperCollins.

Murray, Donald. 1989. *Expecting the Unexpected: Teaching Myself—and Others—to Read and Write.* Portsmouth, NH: Boynton/Cook.

Newkirk, Thomas, with Patricia McLure. 1992. *Listening In: Children Talk About Books (and other things).* Portsmouth, NH: Heinemann.

Nye, Naomi Shihab. 1990. "Valentine for Ernest Mann." In *The Place My Words Are Looking For.* Ed. Paul Janeczko. New York: Bradbury.

———, ed. 1992. *This Same Sky.* New York: Four Winds Press.

Ober, Hal. 1994. *How Music Came to the World.* Boston: Houghton Mifflin.

O'Neill, Mary. 1961, 1989. *Hailstones and Halibut Bones.* New York: Trumpet Club.

Paul, Ann Whitford. 1991. *Eight Hands Round: A Patchwork Alphabet.* New York: HarperCollins.

Peterson, Ralph. 1992. *Life in a Crowded Place: Making a Learning Community.* Portsmouth, NH: Heinemann.

Piercy, Marge. 1989. *Stone, Paper, Knife.* New York: Alfred A. Knopf.

Potter, Beatrix. n.d. *The Tale of Peter Rabbit*. New York: Frederick Warne.

———. 1903. *The Tale of Squirrel Nutkin*. New York: Frederick Warne.

———. 1906. *The Story of a Fierce Bad Rabbit*. New York: Frederick Warne.

Prelutsky, Jack, ed. 1983. *The Random House Book of Poetry for Children*. New York: Random House.

Raboff, Ernest. 1968, 1988. *Paul Klee: Art for Children*. New York: HarperTrophy.

———. 1982. *Pablo Picasso*. New York: Harper and Row.

Raschka, Chris. 1992. *Charlie Parker Played Bebop*. New York: Orchard.

Rief, Linda. 1992. *Seeking Diversity*. Portsmouth, NH: Heinemann.

———. 1995. Reading Writers to Write for Ourselves. Paper presented at the Fall Conference of the National Council of Teachers of English, San Diego, CA.

Ringgold, Faith. 1991. *Tar Beach*. New York: Crown.

Robbins, Ken. 1990. *A Flower Grows*. New York: Dial.

Robinson, Susan. 1989. Mini-Research and Gang Research. Paper presented at the Indiana University Summer Reading Conference, Indianapolis, IN.

Rydell, Katy. 1994. *Wind Says Goodnight*. Boston: Houghton Mifflin.

Sandburg, Carl. 1982. *Rainbows Are Made*. Comp. Lee Bennett Hopkins. San Diego, CA: Harcourt Brace Jovanovich.

Schenk de Regniers, Beatrice, Eva Moore, Mary Michaels White, and Jan Carr, eds. 1988. *Sing a Song of Popcorn*. New York: Scholastic.

Sexton, Anne. 1971. *Transformations*. Boston: Houghton Mifflin.

shange, ntozake. 1994. *i live in music*. Illus. Romare Bearden. New York: Welcome Enterprises.

Shannon, George. 1996. *Tomorrow's Alphabet*. New York: Greenwillow.

Short, Kathy. 1993. Curriculum for the 21st Century: A Redefinition. Paper presented at the National Council of Teachers of English, Pittsburgh, PA.

Shulevitz, Uri. 1974. *Dawn*. New York: Farrar, Straus, and Giroux.

Siebert, Diane. 1988. "Paintings by Wendell Minor." *Mojave*. New York: Thomas Y. Crowell.

Simon, Seymour. 1979. *Animal Fact/Animal Fable* New York: Crown.

———. 1991. "Thoughts on Writing Science Books." In *Vital Connections: Children, Science, and Books*. Ed. Wendy Saul and Sybille A. Jagusch. Portsmouth, NH: Heinemann.

Stafford, William. 1980. *Things That Happen Where There Aren't Any People*. Brockport, NY: BOA Editions.

———. 1992. *The Animal That Drank Up Sound*. Illus. Debra Frasier. New York: Harcourt Brace Jovanovich.

———. 1994. *Learning to Live in the World*. New York: Harcourt Brace.

Stanley, Diane. 1990. *The Conversation Club*. New York: Alladin.

Strickland, Michael, ed. 1993. *Poems That Sing to You*. Honesdale, PA: Boyds Mills Press.

Switzer, Ellen. 1995. *The Magic of Mozart: Mozart, The Magic Flute, and the Salzburg Marionettes*. New York: Atheneum.

Turner, Robyn Montana. 1991. *Georgia O'Keeffe: Portraits of Women Artists for Children*. Boston: Little, Brown.

Upitis, Rena. 1992. *Can I Play You My Song? The Compositions and Invented Notations of Children*. Portsmouth, NH: Heinemann.

Van Maanen, John. 1988. *Tales of the Field: On Writing Ethnography*. Chicago: University of Chicago Press.

Venezia, Mike. 1990. *Mary Cassatt: Getting to Know the World's Greatest Artists*. Chicago: Children's Press.

Viorst, Judith. 1994. *The Alphabet from Z to A (with Much Confusion on the Way)*. New York: Atheneum.

Weigl, Bruce. 1988. *Song of Napalm*. New York: Atlantic Monthly Press.

Whitin, David, and Sandra Wilde. 1992. *Read Any Good Math Lately?* Portsmouth, NH: Heinemann.

Whitman, Walt. 1989. "The Words of the True Poems." In *Imaginary Gardens*. Ed. Charles Sullivan. New York: Harry N. Abrams.

———. 1991. *I Hear America Singing*. New York: Philomel.

Wilks, Mike. 1986. *The Ultimate Alphabet*. London: Michael Joseph.

With Open Eyes. Voyager, New York. CD-ROM.

Woolsey, Daniel, and Frederick Burton. 1986. "Blending Literary and Informational Ways of Knowing." *Language Arts* 63 (3): 274–280.

Wright, James. 1990. *Above the River*. New York: Farrar, Straus, and Giroux.

Yagawa, Sumiko. 1981. *The Crane Wife*. Trans. Katherine Paterson. New York: Mulberry.

Yolen, Jane. 1992. *Letting Swift River Go*. Boston: Little, Brown.

———, ed. 1993. *Weather Report*. Honesdale, PA: Boyds Mills Press.

Poetry Bibliography with Selected Annotations

Books to Get You Started

Adoff, Arnold. 1979. *Eats*. New York: Lothrop, Lee, and Shepard.

———. 1982. *All the Colors of the Race*. New York: Lothrop, Lee, and Shepard.

———. 1986. *Sports Pages*. New York: Harper and Row.

———. 1989. *Chocolate Dreams*. New York: Lothrop, Lee, and Shepard.

———.1991. *Hard to Be Six*. New York: Lothrop, Lee, and Shepard.

Cassedy, Sylvia. 1987. *Roomrimes*. New York: Thomas Y. Crowell.

Chandra, Deborah. 1993. *Rich Lizard and Other Poems*. New York: Farrar, Straus, and Giroux.

Ciardi, John. 1987. *You Read to Me, I'll Read to You*. New York: Harper and Row.

Cole, Joanna, and Stephanie Calmenson. 1990. *Miss Mary Mack and Other Children's Street Rhymes*. New York: William Morrow.

Cooper, Melrose. 1993. *I Got a Family*. New York: Holt.

Dickinson, Emily. 1996. *Poems for Youth*. Boston: Little, Brown.

Dunning, Stephen, Edward Lueders, and Hugh Smith, eds. 1966. *Reflections on a Gift of Watermelon Pickle and Other Modern Verse.* Glenview, IL: Scott Foresman.

Feelings, Tom, ed. 1993. *Soul Looks Back in Wonder.* New York: Dial.

Fleischman, Paul. 1985. *I Am Phoenix: Poems for Two Voices.* New York: Harper and Row.

Fletcher, Ralph. 1991. *Water Planet.* Paramus, NJ: Arrowhead.

Frank, Josette, ed. 1990. *Snow Toward Evening.* New York: Dial.

Frost, Robert. 1959. *You Come Too.* New York: Henry Holt.

———. 1978. *Stopping by Woods on a Snowy Evening.* New York: E. P. Dutton.

———. 1988. *Birches.* New York: Henry Holt.

Giovanni, Nikki. 1996. *The Sun Is So Quiet.* New York: Henry Holt.

Goldstein, Bobbye S., ed. 1992. *Inner Chimes.* Honesdale, PA: Boyds Mills Press.

Greenfield, Eloise. 1988. *Under the Sunday Tree.* New York: Harper and Row.

Heard, Georgia. 1992. *Creatures of Earth, Sea, and Sky.* Honesdale, PA: Boyds Mills Press.

Hopkins, Lee Bennett. 1984. *Surprises.* New York: HarperCollins.

———. 1987. *More Surprises.* New York: Harper and Row.

———, ed. 1990. *Good Books, Good Times!* New York: HarperCollins.

———. 1992. *Questions: Poems of Wonder.* New York: HarperCollins.

———.1996. *Opening Days.* New York: Harcourt Brace.

Hughes, Langston. 1994. *The Dream Keeper and Other Poems.* New York: Alfred A. Knopf.

Janeczko, Paul, ed. 1990. *The Place My Words Are Looking For.* New York: Bradbury.

———, ed. 1994. *Poetry from A to Z.* New York: Bradbury.

Koch, Kenneth, and Kate Farrell, eds. 1985. *Talking to the Sun.* New York: Holt, Rinehart, and Winston.

Kuskin, Karla. 1975. *Near the Window Tree*. New York: Harper and Row.

———. 1992. *Soap Soup and Other Verses*. New York: HarperCollins.

Larrick, Nancy, ed. 1990. *Mice Are Nice*. New York: Philomel.

Lewis, J. Patrick. 1990. *A Hippopotamusn't*. New York: Dial.

Lewis, Richard, ed. 1965. *In a Spring Garden*. New York: Dial.

Livingston, Myra Cohn. 1995. *Call Down the Moon*. New York: Simon and Schuster.

Lobel, Arnold. 1985. *Whiskers and Rhymes*. New York: Mulberry.

Merriam, Eve. 1985. *Blackberry Ink*. New York: William Morrow.

———. 1986. *A Sky Full of Poems*. New York: Dell.

———. 1988. *You Be Good and I'll Be Night*. New York: Morrow.

Myers, Walter Dean. 1993. *Brown Angels: An Album of Pictures and Verse*. New York: HarperCollins.

Nye, Naomi Shihab, ed. 1992. *This Same Sky*. New York: Four Winds Press.

———. 1995. *The Tree Is Older Than You Are*. New York: Simon and Schuster.

O'Neill, Mary. 1961, 1989. *Hailstones and Halibut Bones*. New York: Doubleday.

Panzer, Nora, ed. 1994. *Celebrate America in Poetry and Art*. New York: Hyperion.

Prelutsky, Jack. 1983. *The Random House Book of Poetry for Children*. New York: Random House.

———. 1984. *New Kid on the Block*. New York: Scholastic.

———. 1990. *Something BIG Has Been Here*. New York: Greenwillow.

———, ed. 1991. *For Laughing Out Loud*. New York: Alfred A. Knopf.

Rogasky, Barbara, ed. 1994. *Winter Poems*. New York: Scholastic.

Rosen, Michael. 1995. *The Best of Michael Rosen*. Berkeley, CA: Wetlands Press.

Sandburg, Carl. 1982. *Rainbows Are Made*. Comp. Lee Bennett Hopkins. San Diego, CA: Harcourt Brace Jovanovich.

Schenk de Regniers, Beatrice. 1988. *The Way I Feel Sometimes*. New York: Clarion.

Schenk de Regniers, Beatrice, Eva Moore, Mary Michaels White, and Jan Carr, eds. 1988. *Sing a Song of Popcorn*. New York: Scholastic.

Shannon, George, ed. 1996. *Spring: A Haiku Story*. New York: Greenwillow.

Silverstein, Shel. 1974. *Where the Sidewalk Ends*. New York: Harper and Row.

———. 1981. *A Light in the Attic*. New York: Harper and Row.

———. 1996. *Falling Up*. New York: HarperCollins.

Soto, Gary. 1992. *Neighborhood Odes*. Illus. David Diaz. San Diego, CA: Harcourt Brace Jovanovich.

Stafford, William. 1994. *Learning to Live in the World*. New York: Harcourt Brace.

Sullivan, Charles, ed. 1989. *Imaginary Gardens*. New York: Harry N. Abrams.

Thomas, Joyce Carol. 1993. *Brown Honey in Broomwheat Tea*. Illus. Floyd Cooper. New York: HarperCollins.

Viorst, Judith. 1981. *If I Were in Charge of the World and Other Worries*. New York: Atheneum.

Whipple, Laura, ed. 1994. *Celebrating America*. New York: Philomel.

Worth, Valerie. 1985. *All the Small Poems*. New York: Farrar, Straus, and Giroux.

Yolen, Jane. 1990a. *Bird Watch*. New York: Philomel.

———. 1990b. *Dinosaur Dances*. New York: G. P. Putnam.

———, ed. 1993. *Weather Report*. Honesdale, PA: Boyds Mills Press.

Prose Books with Poetic Imagery

Berger, Barbara. 1990. *Gwinna*. New York: Philomel.

George, Jean Craighead. 1993. *Dear Rebecca, Winter Is Here*. New York: HarperCollins.

Moore, Lillian. 1988. *I'll Meet You at the Cucumbers*. New York: Atheneum.

Siebert, Diane. 1988. *Mojave.* New York: Thomas Y. Crowell.

Teacher Resources

Copeland, Jeffrey S. 1993. *Speaking of Poets: Interviews with Poets Who Write for Children and Young Adults.* Urbana, IL: National Council of Teachers of English.

Copeland, Jeffrey S., and Vicky L. Copeland. 1994. *Speaking of Poets 2: More Interviews with Poets Who Write for Children and Young Adults.* Urbana, IL: National Council of Teachers of English.

These two books include interviews with poets such as Arnold Adoff, Karla Kuskin, Lee Bennett Hopkins, Eve Merriam, and Eloise Greenfield. In the interviews the poets share personal information and talk about their own writing process.

Graves, Donald H. 1992. *Explore Poetry.* Portsmouth, NH: Heinemann.

Through this book Donald Graves encourages readers to experiment with writing poetry. He provides many teaching approaches to try with children.

Heard, Georgia. 1989. *For the Good of the Earth and Sun.* Portsmouth, NH: Heinemann.

A book about the teaching of poetry written by a poet whose passion for what she does comes through clearly.

———. 1995. *Writing Toward Home: Tales and Lessons to Find Your Way.* Portsmouth, NH: Heinemann.

Georgia Heard's words inspire us to take the risks that are inherent in any writing.

Hopkins, Lee Bennett. 1987. *Pass the Poetry, Please!* New York: Harper and Row.

One section in the book acquaints students with poets. Another deals with different kinds of poetry like haiku and concrete poems. The appendices contain annotated titles listed by theme.

Koch, Kenneth. 1973. *Rose, Where Did You Get That Red? Teaching Great Poetry to Children.* New York: Random House.

Kenneth Koch assumes children will respond to the poetry of Walt Whitman, Wallace Stevens, and William Carlos Williams. He helps us use poets like these as mentors.

Livingston, Myra Cohn. 1990. *Climb into the Bell Tower.* New York: Harper and Row.

This book is written as a series of essays. Myra Cohn Livingston opens a window into the world of poets such as David McCord, John Ciardi, and Eve Merriam.

McClure, Amy A., with Peggy Harrison and Sheryl Reed. 1990. *Sunrises and Songs.* Portsmouth, NH: Heinemann.

Amy McClure spent a year visiting Peggy Harrison and Sheryl Reed's multiage fifth- and sixth-grade classroom, enmeshed in the poetry that filled their day. This book is her description of how these two teachers introduce poetry to children and create a love of poetry in their students.

Annotated Bibliography of Books About the Visual Arts

Picture Books That Come to Life

In each of these books the viewer is able to enter into paintings, or subjects step out of paintings to engage the viewer in fascinating conversations. Together they comprise a wonderful text for introducing students to major works of art, and to the artists who created them.

Agee, Jon. 1988. *The Incredible Painting of Felix Clousseau.* New York: Farrar, Straus, and Giroux.

Alcorn, Johnny. 1991. *Rembrandt's Beret.* Illustrated by Stephen Alcorn. New York: Tambourine.

Carrick, Donald. 1985. *Morgan and the Artist.* New York: Clarion.

Demi. 1980. *Liang and the Magic Paintbrush.* New York: Holt, Rinehart, and Winston.

Reiner, Annie. 1990. *A Visit to the Art Galaxy.* San Marcos, CA: Green Tiger Press.

Simmonds, Posy. 1988. *Lulu and the Flying Babies.* New York: Alfred A. Knopf.

Zadrzynska, Ewa. 1990. *The Girl with the Watering Can.* New York: Chameleon.

More Picture Books to Help Generate Excitement

Clement, Claude. 1986. *The Painter and the Wild Swans.* New York: Dial.

Cooney, Barbara. 1990. *Hattie and the Wild Waves*. New York: Viking.

Demi. 1991. *The Artist and the Architect*. New York: Henry Holt.

dePaola, Tomie. 1989. *The Art Lesson*. New York: Trumpet.

———. 1991. *Bonjour, Mr. Satie*. New York: G. P. Putnam.

Johnson, Crockett. 1960. *A Picture for Harold's Room*. New York: Harper.

Johnson, Herschel. 1989. *A Visit to the Country*. Illus. Romare Bearden. New York: Harper and Row.

Locker, Thomas. 1989. *The Young Artist*. New York: Dial.

Ringgold, Faith. 1991. *Tar Beach*. New York: Crown.

Rylant, Cynthia. 1988. *All I See*. Illus. Peter Catalanotto. New York: Orchid.

Strand, Mark. 1986. *Rembrandt Takes a Walk*. Illus. Red Grooms. New York: Clarkson and Potter.

Willard, Nancy. 1991. *Pish, Posh, Said Hieronymus Bosch*. Illus. the Dillons. New York: Harcourt Brace Jovanovich.

Series About Ways of Looking at Works of Art

Come Look with Me Series   Using a question technique Gladys Blizzard helps children develop strategies to look at paintings.

Blizzard, Gladys S. 1990. *Come Look with Me: Enjoying Art with Children*. Charlottesville: Thomasson-Grant.

———. 1992a. *Come Look with Me: Animals in Art*. Charlottesville: Thomasson-Grant.

———. 1992b. *Come Look with Me: Exploring Landscape Art with Children*. Charlottesville: Thomasson-Grant.

———. 1993. *Come Look with Me: World of Play*. Charlottesville: Thomasson-Grant.

First Discovery Art Series   These books are meant to be handled and read by emerging readers. The transparent pages, artfully interspersed in the text, allow children to make discoveries about paintings.

Delafosse, Claude, and Gallimard Jeunesse. 1995a. *Animals.* Trans. Pamela Nelson. New York: Scholastic.

———. 1995b. *Portraits.* Trans. Pamela Nelson. New York: Scholastic.

———. 1996a. *Landscapes.* Trans. Pamela Nelson. New York: Scholastic.

———. 1996b. *Paintings.* Trans. Pamela Nelson. New York: Scholastic.

Looking at Paintings Series   This series explores the unique ways different artists paint the same subjects.

Roalf, Peggy. 1992a. *Dancers: Looking at Paintings.* New York: Hyperion.

———. 1992b. *Families: Looking at Paintings.* New York: Hyperion.

———.1992c. *Seascapes: Looking at Paintings.* New York: Hyperion.

———. 1993a. *Children: Looking at Paintings.* New York: Hyperion.

———. 1993b. *Circus: Looking at Paintings.* New York: Hyperion.

———.1993c. *Flowers: Looking at Paintings.* New York: Hyperion.

———.1993d. *Musicians: Looking at Paintings.* New York: Hyperion.

———.1993e. *Self-portraits: Looking at Paintings.* New York: Hyperion.

The Museum of Modern Art Series   This series introduces the components of painting and sculpture through examples from the Museum of Modern Art in New York. What makes this series particularly attractive is that it is written in an easy to read format.

Yenawine, Philip. 1991a. *Colors. The Museum of Modern Art.* New York: Delacorte.

———. 1991b. *Lines. The Museum of Modern Art.* New York: Delacorte.

———. 1991c. *Shapes. The Museum of Modern Art.* New York: Delacorte.

———. 1991d. *Stories. The Museum of Modern Art.* New York: Delacorte.

———. 1993a. *People. The Museum of Modern Art.* New York: Delacorte.

———. 1993b. *Places. The Museum of Modern Art.* New York: Delacorte.

Series About Artists

Ernest Raboff's Art for Children Series   Written in an accessible style, words are emphasized by using bright colors or enlarging the letters. Quotes from the artists are used in all the books. Full page reproductions are included along with explanations to help understand the paintings.

Raboff, Ernest. 1968, 1988a. *Chagall. Art for Children.* New York: HarperTrophy.

———. 1968, 1988b. *Paul Klee. Art for Children.* New York: HarperTrophy.

———. 1970, 1988a. *Rousseau. Art for Children.* New York: HarperTrophy.

———. 1970, 1988b. *Toulouse-Lautrec. Art for Children.* New York: HarperTrophy.

———. 1971, 1988. *Michelangelo. Art for Children.* New York: HarperTrophy.

———. 1973, 1988. *Van Gogh. Art for Children.* New York: HarperTrophy.

———. 1974, 1988. *Gauguin. Art for Children.* New York: HarperTrophy.

———. 1974. *Velásquez. Art for Children.* New York: Doubleday.

———. 1978, 1988. *Leonardo da Vinci. Art for Children.* New York: HarperTrophy.

———. 1982, 1988. *Picasso. Art for Children.* New York: HarperTrophy.

———. 1988. *Matisse. Art for Children.* New York: HarperTrophy.

Chelsea House Publisher's Art for Children Series   Although written on a more challenging reading level, the Art for Children series includes detailed information about the artist's life. The biographies are embedded in a story narrated by a young boy. Of special interest are the photographs of the artists that are included.

Antoine, Veronique. 1994. *Picasso: A Day in His Studio. Art for Children.* Trans. John Goodman. New York: Chelsea House.

Blanquet, Claire-Helene. 1994. *Miro: Earth and Sky. Art for Children.* Trans. John Goodman. New York: Chelsea House.

Loumaye, Jacqueline. 1994a. *Chagall: My Sad and Joyous Village. Art for Children.* Trans. John Goodman. New York: Chelsea House.

————. 1994b. *Degas: The Painted Gesture. Art for Children.* New York: Chelsea House.

————. 1994c. *Van Gogh: The Touch of Yellow. Art for Children.* New York: Chelsea House.

Pinguilly, Yves. 1994. *Da Vinci: The Painter Who Spoke with Birds. Art for Children.* New York: Chelsea House.

Sterchx, Pierre. 1994. *Brueghel: A Gift for Telling Stories. Art for Children.* New York: Chelsea House.

Art Play Book Series   Even nonreaders can enjoy this series where each book focuses on one painting or sculpture from the collection of the National Museum of Modern Art, Georges Pompidou Center, Paris. Through cutouts, popups, and flipbook pages the art emerges, not revealing itself totally until the end of the book. The books, originally written in French, have been translated into English.

Auge-Amzallag, Elizabeth. 1991. *Henri Matisse: The Sorrowful King. Art Play Books.* Paris: Georges Pompidou Center.

Cvach, Milos, and Sophie Curtil. 1988. *Robert Delaunay: The Eiffel Tower. Art Play Books.* New York: Harry N. Abrams.

de Larminat, Max-Henri. 1990. *Vassily Kandinsky: Sky Blue. Art Play Books.* New York: Harry N. Abrams.

Giraudy, Daniele. 1987. *Pablo Picasso: The Minotaur. Art Play Books.* Paris: Georges Pompidou Center.

Prats-Okuyama, Catherine, and Kimihito Okuyama. 1987. *Dubuffet: Le Jardin d'Hiver. Art Play Books.* Paris: Georges Pompidou Center.

The Eyewitness Art Series   These books are written in association with one particular art museum. For example, *Perspective* includes many paintings from the National Gallery collection in London. The books are packed with excellent reproductions, information, and interesting anecdotes. These books can be used as a whole to give a greater understanding of a subject like impressionism. Parts of the books can be used when a student wants to focus on a specific artist.

Bernard, Bruce. 1992. *Van Gogh. Eyewitness Art.* London: Dorling Kindersley.

Clarke, Michael. 1993. *Watercolor. Eyewitness Art.* London: Dorling Kindersley.

Cole, Alison. 1992. *Perspective. Eyewitness Art.* London: Dorling Kindersley/ National Gallery.

———. 1994. *The Renaissance. Eyewitness Art.* London: Dorling Kindersley/ National Gallery.

Howard, Michael. 1992. *Gauguin. Eyewitness Art.* London: Dorling Kindersley and Tahiti: Musée Gauguin.

Welton, Jude. 1992. *Monet. Eyewitness Art.* London: Dorling Kindersley and Paris: Musée Marmottan.

———. 1993. *Impressionism. Eyewitness Art.* London: Dorling Kindersley and Chicago: The Art Institute of Chicago.

———. 1994. *Looking at Paintings. Eyewitness Art.* London: Dorling Kindersley/National Gallery.

Wiggins, Colin. 1993. *Post-Impressionism. Eyewitness Art.* London: Dorling Kindersley and Chicago: The Art Institute of Chicago.

Wright, Patricia. 1993a. *Goya. Eyewitness Art.* London: Dorling Kindersley/ National Gallery.

———. 1993b. *Manet. Eyewitness Art.* London: Dorling Kindersley.

First Impressions Series These biographies are written for independent readers who want to find out the smallest details about a particular artist.

Berman, Avis. 1993. *James McNeill Whistler. First Impressions.* New York: Harry N. Abrams.

Greenfeld, Howard. 1990. *Marc Chagall: First Impressions.* New York: Harry N. Abrams.

———. 1993. *Paul Gauguin: First Impressions.* New York: Harry N. Abrams.

Meryman, Richard. 1991. *Andrew Wyeth: First Impressions.* New York: Harry N. Abrams.

Meyer, Susan E. 1990. *Mary Cassatt: First Impressions.* New York: Harry N. Abrams.

———. 1994. *Edgar Degas: First Impressions.* New York: Harry N. Abrams.

Waldron, Ann. 1991. *Claude Monet: First Impressions.* New York: Harry N. Abrams.

———. 1992. *Francisco Goya: First Impressions.* New York: Harry N. Abrams.

Mike Venezia's Getting to Know the World's Greatest Artists Series One of the easiest for kids to read, this series is written in a very breezy style with a sense of humor conveyed by cartoons and word balloons. Artists are presented as real people.

Venezia, Mike. 1988a. *Da Vinci. Getting to Know the World's Greatest Artists.* Chicago: Children's Press.

———. 1988b. *Picasso. Getting to Know the World's Greatest Artists.* Chicago: Children's Press.

———. 1988c. *Rembrandt. Getting to Know the World's Greatest Artists.* Chicago: Children's Press.

———. 1988d. *Van Gogh. Getting to Know the World's Greatest Artists.* Chicago: Children's Press.

———. 1990a. *Edward Hopper. Getting to Know the World's Greatest Artists.* Chicago: Children's Press.

———. 1990b. *Mary Cassatt. Getting to Know the World's Greatest Artists.* Chicago: Children's Press.

———. 1990c. *Monet. Getting to Know the World's Greatest Artists.* Chicago: Children's Press.

———. 1991a. *Goya. Getting to Know the World's Greatest Artists.* Chicago: Children's Press.

———. 1991b. *Michelangelo. Getting to Know the World's Greatest Artists.* Chicago: Children's Press.

Introducing . . . Series Another series designed for independent readers, *Introducing . . .* is filled with many reproductions of artwork and photographs. It also supplies answers to questions that it assumes the readers have.

Heslewood, Juliet. 1993. *Introducing Picasso.* Boston: Little, Brown.

Richmond, Robin. 1992. *Introducing Michelangelo: Sculptor, Painter, Poet.* Boston: Little, Brown.

Sturgis, Alexander. 1994. *Introducing Rembrandt.* Boston: Little, Brown.

Portraits of Women Artists for Children Series   Robyn Montana Turner decided to write this series of books about women artists because she realized that many of the biographies about women were designed for an adult audience. She wanted children to be able to discover female artists, so she describes how women overcome obstacles to achieve a career in art in these moving and involving stories.

Turner, Robyn Montana. 1991a. *Georgia O'Keeffe: Portraits of Women Artists for Children.* Boston: Little, Brown.

———. 1991b. *Rosa Bonheur: Portraits of Women Artists for Children.* Boston: Little, Brown.

———. 1992. *Mary Cassatt: Portraits of Women Artists for Children.* Boston: Little, Brown.

———. 1993a. *Faith Ringgold: Portraits of Women Artists for Children.* Boston: Little, Brown.

———. 1993b. *Frida Kahlo: Portraits of Women Artists for Children.* Boston: Little, Brown.

A Weekend with . . . Series   In these books the artist talks to the reader in the first person. The reader is the weekend guest in the artist's home. The illusion is so complete that at the end of *A Weekend with Picasso* you believe that Picasso is putting a costume on "you," the person he's been talking to through the book.

Beneduce, Ann Keay. 1993. *A Weekend with Winslow Homer.* New York: Rizzoli.

Bonafoux, Pascal. 1992. *A Weekend with Rembrandt.* New York: Rizzoli.

Plazy, Gilles. 1993. *A Weekend with Rousseau.* New York: Rizzoli.

Rodari, Florian. 1991. *A Weekend with Picasso.* New York: Rizzoli.

———. 1993. *A Weekend with Velázquez.* New York: Rizzoli.

———. 1994. *A Weekend with Matisse.* New York: Rizzoli.

Skira-Venturi, Rosabianca. 1990. *A Weekend with Renoir.* New York: Rizzoli.

————. 1991. *A Weekend with Degas.* New York: Rizzoli.

What Makes a . . . a . . .? Series   How can you recognize a particular artist's work? What makes it clear that *Cypresses* could only have been painted by Van Gogh or that *Water Lilies* was painted by Monet? Sections of paintings are enlarged in order to focus on color, composition, or brushwork. For children who are trying to work in the style of a particular artist this book is very help-ful. Independent readers will be able to make sense of the text. Nonreaders will find the reproductions of the artwork with enlargements of small areas very useful.

Muhlberger, Richard. 1993a. *What Makes a Bruegel a Bruegel? Metropolitan Museum of Art.* New York: Viking.

————. 1993b. *What Makes a Degas a Degas? Metropolitan Museum of Art.* New York: Viking.

————. 1993c. *What Makes a Monet a Monet? Metropolitan Museum of Art.* New York: Viking.

————. 1993d. *What Makes a Raphael a Raphael? Metropolitan Museum of Art.* New York: Viking.

————. 1993e. *What Makes a Rembrandt a Rembrandt? Metropolitan Museum of Art.* New York: Viking.

————. 1993f. *What Makes a Van Gogh a Van Gogh? Metropolitan Museum of Art.* New York: Viking.

Biographies of Artists

Bjork, Christina, and Lena Anderson. 1987. *Linnea in Monet's Garden.* New York: Farrar, Straus, and Giroux.

Corsi, Jerome R. 1995. *Leonardo da Vinci.* Rohnert Park, CA: Pomegranate Artbooks.

Everett, Gwen. 1991. *Li'l Sis and Uncle Willie: A Story Based on the Life and Paintings of William H. Johnson.* New York: Rizzoli.

Grooms, Red. 1988. *Ruckus Rodeo.* New York: Harry N. Abrams.

Kalman, Maira. 1991. *Roarr: Calder's Circus*. Photo. Donatella Brun. New York: Whitney Museum of Modern Art.

Lipman, Jean, with Margaret Aspinwall. 1981. *Alexander Calder and His Magical Mobiles*. New York: Hudson Hills Press.

Munthe, Nelly. 1983. *Meet Matisse*. Boston: Little, Brown.

Newlands, Anne. 1988. *Meet Edgar Degas*. Toronto: Kids Can Press.

Sills, Leslie. 1989. *Inspirations: Stories About Women Artists*. Niles, IL: Albert Whitman. (Biographies of Georgia O'Keeffe, Frida Kahlo, Alice Neel, and Faith Ringgold)

———. 1993. *Visions: Stories About Women Artists*. Niles, IL: Albert Whitman. (Biographies of Mary Cassatt, Betye Saar, Leonora Carrington, and Mary Frank)

Poetry and Art

Koch, Kenneth, and Kate Farrell, eds. 1985. *Talking to the Sun*. New York: Holt, Rinehart, and Winston.

Panzer, Nora, ed. 1994. *Celebrate America in Poetry and Art*. New York: Hyperion.

Sullivan, Charles, ed. 1989. *Imaginary Gardens*. New York: Harry N. Abrams.

———. 1991. *Children of Promise: African American Literature and Art for Young People*. New York: Harry N. Abrams.

Whipple, Laura, ed. 1994. *Celebrating America*. New York: Philomel.

Color

Ardley, Neil. 1991. *The Science Book of Color*. San Diego: Harcourt Brace Jovanovich.
Experiments involving color are outlined using an easy to read format. The directions for all the experiments include helpful photographs showing kids doing the actual work.

Goffstein, M. B. 1987. *Artists' Helpers Enjoy the Evening*. New York: Harper and Row.

Jonas, Ann. 1989. *Color Dance*. New York: Greenwillow.

Taylor, Barbara. 1992. *Over the Rainbow! The Science of Color and Light. Step into Science*. New York: Random House.

Introduction to an Art Museum

Levy, Virginia. 1983. *Let's Go to the Art Museum*. New York: Harry N. Abrams.

Book, Music, and Video Resources for the Classroom

Stories About Music

Ackerman, Karen. 1988. *Song and Dance Man*. New York: Alfred A. Knopf.

Bottner, Barbara. 1987. *Zoo Song*. New York: Scholastic.

Brett, Jan. 1991. *Berlioz the Bear*. New York: G. P. Putnam.

Cherry, Lynne. 1992. *A River Ran Wild*. New York: Harcourt Brace Jovanovich.

Ewart, Claire. 1992. *One Cold Night*. New York: G. P. Putnam.

Fleischman, Paul. 1988. *Rondo in C*. New York: Harper and Row.

Hurd, Thatcher. 1984. *Mama Don't Allow*. New York: Harper and Row.

Isadora, Rachel. 1979. *Ben's Trumpet*. New York: Greenwillow.

Komaiko, Leah. 1989. *I Like the Music*. New York: HarperTrophy.

Kuskin, Karla. 1982. *The Philharmonic Gets Dressed*. New York: Harper and Row.

Martin, Bill Jr., and John Archambault. 1986. *Barn Dance*. New York: Henry Holt.

Maxner, Joyce. 1989. *Nicholas Cricket*. New York: Harper and Row.

Moss, Lloyd. 1995. *Zin! Zin! Zin! A Violin*. Illus. Marjorie Priceman. New York: Simon and Schuster.

McKissack, Patricia. 1988. *Mirandy and Brother Wind*. Illus. Jerry Pinkney. New York: Alfred A. Knopf.

Ober, Hal. 1994. *How Music Came to the World*. Boston: Houghton Mifflin.

Rydell, Katy. 1994. *Wind Says Good Night*. Boston: Houghton Mifflin.

van Kampen, Vlasta, and Irene C. Eugen. 1989. *Orchestranimals*. New York: Scholastic.

Weiss, George, and Bob Thiele. 1995. *What a Wonderful World*. Illus. Ashley Bryan. New York: Atheneum.

Yagawa, Sumiko. 1981. *The Crane Wife*. Trans. Katherine Paterson. New York: Mulberry.

Yolen, Jane. 1992. *Letting Swift River Go*. Boston: Little, Brown.

Nonfiction Books About Music

Ardley, Neil. 1989. *Music. Eyewitness Books*. New York: Alfred A. Knopf.

Cornelissen, Cornelia. 1995. *Music in the Wood*. Photo. John Maclachlan. New York: Delacorte.

Danes, Emma. 1993. *The Usborne First Book Of Music: A Complete Introduction*. London: Usborne Publishing Ltd.

Hawkinson, John, and Martha Faulhaber. 1969. *Music and Instruments for Children to Make*. New York: Albert Whitman.

Hausherr, Rosmarie. 1992. *What Instrument Is This?* New York: Scholastic.

Hughes, Langston. 1976. *The First Book of Jazz*. New York: Franklin Watts.

———. 1995. *The Book of Rhythms*. New York: Oxford University Press.

Jackson, Mike. 1993. *Making Music: Shake, Rattle, and Roll with Instruments You Make Yourself*. New York: HarperCollins.

Merlion Arts Library. 1992. *Beating the Drum, Flutes, Reeds, and Trumpets;* and *Rattles, Bells, and Chiming Bars*. Chippenham, UK: Merlion Publishing Ltd.

Paxton, Arthur K. 1986. *Making Music*. New York: Atheneum.

Rubin, Mark, and Alan Daniel. 1984. *The Orchestra*. Toronto, ONT: Douglas and McIntyre.

Roalf, Peggy. 1993. *Musicians: Looking at Paintings*. New York: Hyperion.

Scholastic Voyages of Discovery. 1994. *Musical Instruments*. New York: Scholastic.

Biographies of Musicians

Brighton, Catherine. 1990. *Mozart: Scenes from the Childhood of the Great Composer*. New York: Doubleday.

Downing, Julie. 1991. *Mozart Tonight*. New York: Bradbury.

Goffstein, M. B. 1984. *A Little Schubert*. New York: Trumpet.

Krull, Kathleen. 1993. *Lives of the Musicians: Good Times, Bad Times (And What the Neighbors Thought)*. Orlando: Harcourt Brace Jovanovich.

Lepscky, Ibi. 1992. *Amadeus Mozart*. Hauppauge, NY: Barron's Educational Series.

Medearis, Angela Shelf. 1994. *Little Louis and the Jazz Band: The Story of Louis "Satchmo" Armstrong*. New York: Lodestar Books.

Mitchell, Barbara. 1987. *America, I Hear You: A Story About George Gershwin*. Minneapolis: Carolrhoda Books.

Monceaux, Morgan. 1994. *Jazz: My Music, My People*. New York: Alfred A. Knopf.

Monjo, F. N. 1991. *Letters to Horseface: Young Mozart's Travels in Italy*. New York: Puffin.

Nichols, Barbara. 1993. *Beethoven Lives Upstairs*. New York: Orchard.

Rachlin, Ann. 1993. *Famous Children: Chopin*. London: Alladin.

Raschka, Chris. 1992. *Charlie Parker Played Bebop*. New York: Orchard.

Schroeder, Alan. 1989. *Ragtime Tumpie*. Boston: Little, Brown.

Simon, Charnan. 1992. *Seiji Ozawa Symphony Conductor*. Chicago: Children's Press.

Stevens, Bryna. 1990. *Handel and the Famous Sword Swallower of Halle*. New York: Philomel.

Venezia, Mike. 1994. *Getting to Know the World's Greatest Composers: George Gershwin*. Chicago: Children's Press.

Ventura, Pietro. 1988. *Great Composers*. New York: G. P. Putnam.

Weil, Lisl. 1991. *Wolferel: The First Six Years in the Life of Wolfgang Amadeus Mozart (1756–1762)*. New York: Holiday House.

Opera Stories

Medearis, Angela Shelf. 1995. *Treemonisha*. From the opera by Scott Joplin. New York: Henry Holt.

Price, Leontyne. 1990. *Aida*. New York: Harcourt Brace Jovanovich.

Switzer, Ellen. 1995. *The Magic of Mozart: Mozart, The Magic Flute, and The Salzburg Marionettes*. New York: Atheneum.

Thee, Christian. 1994. *Behind the Curtain: Hansel and Gretel*. New York: Workman.

Stories About Dance

Anholt, Laurence. 1996. *Degas and the Little Dancer*. Hauppauge, NY: Barron's Educational Series.

Chappell, Warren. 1981. *Peter and the Wolf: With Themes from the Music by Serge Prokofieff*. New York: Schocken.

Fonteyn, Margot. 1989. *Swan Lake*. New York: Harcourt Brace Jovanovich.

Gauch, Patricia Lee. 1989. *Dance, Tanya*. New York: Philomel.

Gray, Libba Moore. 1995. *My Mama Had a Dancing Heart*. New York: Orchard.

Helprin, Mark. 1989. *Swan Lake*. Boston: Houghton Mifflin.

Holabird, Katharine. 1983. *Angelina Ballerina*. New York: Puffin.

Isadora, Rachel. 1976. *Max*. New York: Macmillan.

———. 1991. *Swan Lake*. New York: G. P. Putnam.

Locker, Thomas. 1997. *Water Dance*. New York: Harcourt Brace.

Prokofiev, Sergi. 1986. *Peter and the Wolf*. Scenes by Barbara Cooney. New York: Viking Penguin.

Ryder, Joanne. 1996. *Earth Dance*. New York: Henry Holt.

Schick, Eleanor. 1992. *I Have Another Language: The Language Is Dance*. New York: Macmillan.

Simon, Carly. 1989. *Amy the Dancing Bear*. New York: Doubleday.

Thomas, Annabel. 1986. *An Usborne Guide: Ballet*. London: Usborne Publishing Ltd.

Verdy, Violette. 1991. *Of Swans, Sugarplums, and Satin Slippers: Ballet Stories for Children*. New York: Scholastic.

Biographies of Dancers

Barboza, Steven. 1992. *I Feel Like Dancing: A Year with Jacques d'Amboise and the National Dance Institute*. New York: Crown.

Brighton, Catherine. 1989. *Nijinsky: Scenes from the Childhood of the Great Dancer*. New York: Doubleday.

Kristy, Davida. 1996. *George Balanchine: American Ballet Master*. Minneapolis: Lerner.

Pinkney, Andrea Davis, and Brian Pinkney. 1993. *Alvin Ailey*. New York: Hyperion.

Tobias, Paul. 1970. *Maria Tallchief*. New York: Thomas Y. Crowell.

Tobias, Tobi. 1975. *Arthur Mitchell*. New York: Thomas Y. Crowell.

Poetry About Music and Dance
The poetry books listed below are excellent for helping students of all ages internalize the rhythms of language.

Bryan, Ashley. 1992. *Sing to the Sun*. New York: HarperCollins.

Fleischman, Paul. 1988. *Joyful Noise: Poems for Two Voices*. New York: Harper and Row.

Giovanni, Nikki. 1971. *Spin a Soft Black Song*. New York: Farrar, Straus, and Giroux.

Greenfield, Eloise. 1978. *Honey, I Love and Other Love Poems*. New York: Thomas Y. Crowell.

———. 1988. *Nathaniel Talking*. New York: Black Butterfly.

Heard, Georgia. 1992. *Creatures of Earth, Sea, and Sky*. Honesdale, PA: Boyds Mills Press.

Hopkins, Lee Bennett, ed. 1983. *The Sky Is Full of Song*. New York: HarperCollins.

Hughes, Langston. 1994. *The Dream Keeper and Other Poems*. New York: Alfred A. Knopf.

Lewis, Richard. 1991. *All of You Was Singing*. New York: Atheneum.

Martin, Bill Jr., and John Archambault. 1988. *Listen to the Rain*. New York: Henry Holt.

shange, ntozake. 1994. *i live in music*. Illus. Romare Bearden. New York: Welcome Enterprises.

Strickland, Michael R., ed. 1993. *Poems That Sing to You*. Honesdale, PA: Boyds Mills Press.

Whitman, Walt. 1991. *I Hear America Singing*. New York: Philomel.

Yolen, Jane. 1995. *Water Music*. Honesdale, PA: Boyds Mills Press.

Professional References for Teachers

Eisner, Elliot. 1994. *Cognition and Curriculum Reconsidered*. 2d ed. New York: Teachers College Press.

This is one of the most accessible discussions of the importance of extending meaning making to include the sign systems of music, dance, and the visual arts. Eisner's focus is on developing multiliterate students.

Copeland, Jeffrey S., and Vicky L. Copeland. 1995. *Speaking of Poets 2: More Interviews with Poets Who Write for Children and Young Adults*. Urbana, IL: National Council of Teachers of English.

Many of the poets interviewed for this book talk about the ways they search for the music in language when creating a poem. Great teacher resource book.

Finckel, Edwin A., ed. 1993. *Now We'll Make the Rafters Ring: Classic and Contemporary Rounds for Everyone*. Chicago: A Cappella.

Rounds are an excellent way to help children build and maintain focusing skills. This book is full of rounds for all age levels from simple to complex.

Gottlieb, Jack, ed. 1992. *Leonard Bernstein's Young People's Concerts*. New York: Doubleday.

Invaluable resource for teachers and students of all ages. The editor has compiled transcripts from Bernstein's unique television series, each dealing with intriguing questions about the world of music, and each supported by a specific piece of music.

Haas, Karl. 1984. *Inside Music: How to Understand, Listen to, and Enjoy Good Music.* New York: Doubleday.

The world of classical music can be quite intimidating to the novice. Karl Haas (of *Adventures in Good Music* radio fame) makes that world much more accessible through his clear discussions of major pieces of music.

Hart, Avery, and Paul Mantell. 1993. *Kids Make Music! Clapping and Tapping from Bach to Rock!* Charlotte, VT: Williamson.

Great resource book for teachers with interesting lessons on everything from how to write invented notation to making simple instruments.

Hughes, Langston. 1995. *The Book of Rhythms.* New York: Oxford University Press.

The foreword by Wynton Marsalis is a gem. Langston Hughes has written a book for children about his deep feelings for music, but it is filled with ideas for teachers as well.

Kirby, Dan, and Carol Kuykendall. 1991. *Mind Matters: Teaching for Thinking.* Portsmouth, NH: Boynton/Cook.

Anyone interested in developing workshop environments for students must read this book. It helps teachers see how they might create the worlds of the archeologist, inventor, naturalist, or creative artist within the classroom.

Painter, William M. 1994. *Storytelling with Music, Puppets, and Arts for Libraries and Classrooms.* North Haven, CT: The Shoe String Press.

An innovative book that is full of suggestions for enhancing language with music. Suggestions for specific pieces make this a valuable resource for the teacher new to teaching through the arts.

Videos

An Evening with the Alvin Ailey American Dance Theatre. 1986. Chicago: RM Arts/DR/Musikafdelingen.

A celebration of the choreography of the Alvin Ailey American Dance Theatre, this videocassette contains *Revelations*, the signature piece of Alvin

Ailey's career. Showing *Revelations* after reading Andrea and Brian Pinkney's biography of Alvin Ailey will truly bring the man's work to life for students.

Baryshnikov: The Dancer and the Dance. 1983. Long Branch, NJ: Kultur International Films.

A rare opportunity to get inside the head of a gifted dancer and an equally gifted choreographer as we follow the creation of a ballet from beginning to end. Excellent background for teachers, it can be used with students of all ages when talking about dance, composing, interpreting music, or following the evolution of a work.

Bergman, Ingmar. 1986. *Ingmar Bergman's The Magic Flute.* Hollywood: Bel Canto Paramount Home Video.

A story within a story, this is a whimsical retelling of *The Magic Flute*, complete with hot air balloons.

Dancing for Mr. B: Six Balanchine Ballerinas. 1995. Anne Belle. New York: Seahorse Films.

A look at Balanchine's genius as interpreted by such famous Balanchine ballerinas as Maria Tallchief, Melissa Hayden, and Allegra Kent. Archival video clips and interviews with the ballerinas provide fascinating background knowledge for anyone interested in learning about ballet.

Fantasia. Walt Disney Studios. Burbank, CA: Buena Vista Home Video.

Excellent for helping children understand how sound can be turned into images, from simple shapes and colors to complete stories such as *The Sorcerer's Apprentice* or the animated story of Beethoven's Sixth Symphony (*The Pastoral*). This tape contains music and scenes for many of the lessons described in Chapter 6.

Glynbourne Opera Festival. 1985. *Mozart's The Magic Flute.* New York: Video Arts International.

Excellent version of this opera with Kathleen Battle singing the role of Pamina.

Marsalis, Wynton. 1995. Marsalis on Music. Sony Music Entertainment.

———. 1995a. *Listening for Clues.* Sony Music Entertainment. SHV 66489.

———. 1995b. *Sousa to Satchmo.* Sony Music Entertainment. SHV 66490.

———. 1995c. *Tackling the Monster.* Sony Music Entertainment. SHV 66312.

————. 1995d. *Why Toes Tap.* Sony Music Entertainment. SHV 66488.

This is a wonderful set of videos that can serve as an excellent resource for teachers and students alike. Wynton Marsalis combines his extensive knowledge of music with the work of the students at Tanglewood Music Center to create rich and informative lessons on various aspects of music.

On the Day You Were Born. 1996. Read by author Debra Frasier. Featuring the Minnesota Orchestra. Music by Steve Heitzeg. Conducted by William Eddins. Notes Alive! Story Concert Series. Minnesota Orchestra Visual Entertainment. Videocassette.

A story concert with three-dimensional animation and original music, this video combines story, artwork, and music into an unforgettable experience.

Solti, Sir George, and Dudley Moore. 1991a. *Orchestra!: Brass, Percussion.* London: Decca Recording Company.

————. 1991b. *Orchestra! Introduction to the Orchestra, Upper Strings, Woodwinds.* London: Decca Recording Company.

————. 1991c. *Orchestra!: Piano, Conductor, the Making of Orchestra.* London: Decca Recording Company.

Conductor Sir Georg Solti and actor/classical pianist Dudley Moore (playing it straight as a musician) have collaborated to create this series of videotapes about the structure of a symphony orchestra. A combination of conversation and performance make these a rare find for teachers to use as educational background for themselves and/or students.

Tribute to Alvin Ailey. 1990. R. M. Arts. Public Home Video.

The energy and creativity of Alvin Ailey's choreography is captured in a range of works, including an unforgettable interpretation of jazz great Charlie Parker's "Night In Tunisia." Use to enhance the reading of Andrea Davis Pinkney's *Alvin Ailey,* or Chris Raschka's *Charlie Parker Played Bebop.*

Some Musical Possibilities for the Classroom

Books Paired with Music

Ben's Trumpet by Rachel Isadora / *Miles Davis Collection: A Retrospective* with Miles Davis

Charlie Parker Played Bebop by Chris Raschka/"Night in Tunisia" played by Charlie Parker

Dawn by Uri Shulevitz/*Sunrise* Movement from Grofé's *Grand Canyon Suite*

Dreamkeepers by Langston Hughes/*Coltrane Plays the Blues* with John Coltrane

Listen to the Rain by Bill Martin Jr./*Cloudburst* Movement from Grofé's *Grand Canyon Suite*

Mama Don't Allow by Thatcher Hurd/*Hush* with Bobby McFerrin and Yo Yo Ma

Mirandy and Brother Wind by Patricia McKissack/*Cakewalk* from *Piano Rags of Scott Joplin*

Rondo in C by Paul Fleischman/*Rondo in C* by Ludwig von Beethoven

Treemonisha by Angela Shelf Medearis/excerpts from the cast recording of the opera *Treemonisha*

Water Music by Jane Yolen/*Water Music* by George Frideric Handel

What a Wonderful World by George Weiss and Bob Thiele with paintings by Ashley Bryan/"What a Wonderful World" from *Louis Armstrong's Greatest Hits* compact disc by Louis Armstrong

The following two sections are particularly good for translating music into writing, drawing, or dance.

Music That Evokes Strong Images

These pieces work well for interpretation through drawing, writing, or movement.

Four Seasons by Antonio Vivaldi

In the Hall of the Mountain Kings by Edvard Grieg

Night on Bald Mountain by Igor Stravinsky

Toccata and Fugue by Johann Sebastian Bach

Carnival of the Animals by Camille Saint-Saens

Environment and Setting

An American in Paris by George Gershwin

Appalachian Spring by Aaron Copland

La Mer by Claude Debussy

Pictures at an Exhibition by Modest Mussorgsky

Sunset Movement from *Grand Canyon Suite* by Grofé

Rodeo by Aaron Copland

Mirroring

Adagio for Strings by Samuel Barber

Canon in D by Pachelbel

Adagietto from Symphony No. 10 by Gustav Mahler

Additional Compact Discs and Audiocassettes

Bach, Johann Sebastian. *Brandenburg Concertos Nos. 1, 2, and 3.* Boston Baroque. Martin Pearlman. Telarc compact disc BIT CD-80368.

Ballet Music from Coppelia, Sylvia, and Faust. Paris Opera Orchestra. Roberto Benzi. Polygram Classics audiocassette 411 177-4.

Beethoven, Ludwig van. *Symphonie No. 6 Pastorale.* Wiener Philharmoniker. Leonard Bernstein. Deutsche Grammophon compact disc 413 779-2.

The audio version of the symphony can be used to visualize settings, to choregraph dance, and to review the animated story from *Fantasia.*

Beethoven, Ludwig van. *Symphony No. 7.* The Cleveland Orchestra. George Szell. Columbia Odyssey audiocassette 34624.

The Third Movement of this symphony is one of the best pieces of music for learning about patterns from the inside out (see Chapter 2).

Classics for Children. The Boston Pops Orchestra. Arthur Fiedler. RCA Victor audiocassette 68131-4.

Includes *Carnival of the Animals,* one of the best pieces for interpretation of music either through art or dance.

Debussy, Claude. *Complete Orchestral Works.* Orchestra National de l'O.R.T.F. Jean Martinon. EMI compact disc CDM 7 69589 2.

Excellent for visualizing music, this disc includes pieces such as *The Snow Is Dancing.* We often have the students quick-sketch while listening.

Familiar Music for Family Fun. The Boston Pops Orchestra. Arthur Fiedler. RCA Victrola audiocassette ALK1-5383.

This tape includes the *Bach Little Fugue* which is excellent for interpreting pattern, and the *Flight of the Bumblebee*, which is wonderful for visualizing music.

Fantasia. The Philadelphia Orchestra. Leopold Stokowski. Visa two-volume set audiocassette 60074.

Mozart. Wolfgang Amadeus. *Mozart: The Greatest Hits.* Two compact disc set. Reference Gold RGD3603.

———. *The Magic Flute.* Berlin Philharmonic Orchestra. Karl Bohm. Deutsche Grammaphon compact disc 429 825-2.

The Overture and excerpts from the opera can be played as an enhancement to the reading of the story, and as a way of studying characters through music.

Mussorgsky, Modest. *Pictures at an Exhibition.* The New Philharmonic Orchestra. Leopold Stokowski. London Treasury audiocassette 417 087-4.

Use before a trip to the art museum for visualizing a setting or for setting the stage for writing or drawing.

Nikai, R. Carlos. *Canyon Trilogy.* Native American Flute Music. Canyon Records Production compact disc CR-610.

Flute music on this CD is excellent for helping students get a feel for the landscape and mood of the desert. Use when studying the environment or when highlighting Native Americans.

O'Donnell, Eugene. *Slow Airs and Set Dances.* Green Linnet Records, Inc., compact disc GLCD 1015.

(The) Orchestra. Peter Ustinov and the Toronto Philharmonia Orchestra. MRP Records compact disc MRPCD107.

Excellent teaching CD which pairs information about each section of the orchestra with a piece of music that illustrates the lesson. Great resource for teachers.

Perlman, Itzhak. *In the Fiddler's House.* Angel compact disc 7243-5 55555 2 6.

Prokofiev, Serge. *Peter and the Wolf* narrated by Sting. The Chamber Orchestra of Europe. Claudio Abbado. Deutsche Grammophon audiocassette 429 396-4.

Tchaikovsky, Pyotor. *Swan Lake and Sleeping Beauty.* The New Philharmonic Orchestra. Leopold Stokowski. London Treasury audiocassette 410 105-4.

Vincent Van Gogh: Pictures in Music. Claude Debussy and Maurice Ravel. BMG Classics compact disc 60693-2-RG.

In this unique CD the impressionist works of Vincent Van Gogh are looked at in terms of the impressionist music of Claude Debussy and Maurice Ravel.

Vivaldi, Antonio. *The Four Seasons.* Itzhak Perlman. Israel Philharmonic Orchestra. EMI Angel audiocassette 4DS-38123.

Use the music to celebrate the beginning of each season, to visualize music, or to bring the study of science alive (see Chapter 2).

Winter, Paul. *Concert for the Earth.* Living Music compact disc LD-0005.

———. *Canyon.* Living Music compact disc LMRCD-6.

Both Paul Winter CDs are excellent for helping students visualize an environment and are an effective enhancement to a study of the environment.

Yo Yo Ma and Bobby McFerrin. *Hush.* Sony Masterworks compact disc SK 48177.

Excellent for helping students see that the voice is truly a musical instrument.